Benjamin I. Guenther

Day Trade for a Living

"Starter Pack for beginners"

2020 Edition

Trading Strategies & Tactics to
Consistently Earn Passive Income
in Any Market-Stocks, Forex,
Bitcoin, Crypto, CFDs, Futures,
Bonds

Contents

What is Forex?

If we lived in a world where there was only one currency, there would be no foreign exchange market or fluctuating rates; but that's not how our world works. Instead we have primarily national currencies, and the foreign exchange market is an essential mechanism for making payments across country borders.

The foreign exchange market creates a way to transfer funds between countries and to purchase things in other counties. In this chapter, we look at what the foreign exchange market is and who trades foreign currency.

What is Forex?

Forex is actually a short way of saying foreign exchange currency trading. Today the Forex market is by far the largest and most liquid market in the world.

On average more than US$2 trillion is traded each day in the foreign exchange market.

Not only is the total volume hard to fathom for most people, the sheer volume of some individual trades can involve much more money than most people deal with in their entire lifetimes. It's not uncommon to hear of individual trades in the US$200 million to US$500 million range.

It's a fast-moving market, too. Price quotes for a currency pair can change as often as 20 times a minute, or every 3 seconds. The most active exchange rates can change up to 18,000 times during a single day. Actual price movements tend to be in relatively small increments, which also makes this a smoothly functioning and liquid market.

Foreign currency is exchanged in financial centers around the world, but the largest amount of currency actually changes hands in the United Kingdom. Well, changing hands may not be a good metaphor, because most of the transactions are done by electronic transmission, and paper currency is not really moved from one trader to another. Instead, an initial trade of foreign currency with one dealer leads to a number of different transactions over several days as various financial institutions readjusts their positions (the open trades held by a trader).

Where do most foreign exchanges take place? About 32 percent of all currency trades are handled through financial institutions in the United Kingdom, even though the British

pound is not as widely traded as some of the other key currencies, such as the U.S. dollar, the euro, the Japanese yen, and the Swiss franc. U.S. financial institutions rank second in the volume of foreign exchange transactions handled, but that's a distant second—just 18 percent of foreign exchange transactions are handled by U.S. institutions. Japanese financial institutions rank third, with 8 percent of the transactions passing through their doors. Singapore is a close fourth, with 7 percent.

The United Kingdom is the most active financial trading center because of London's strong position as the international financial center of the world, where a large number of financial headquarters are located.

According to a foreign exchange turnover survey, more than 200 foreign exchange dealer institutions in the United Kingdom reported trading activity to the Bank of England, whereas only 93 in the United States were reporting to the United States Federal Reserve Bank of New York.

London has a major advantage over U.S. markets because of its geographic location. Because it is in the center (in regard to its time zone), the normal business hours for London financial institutions coincide with other world financial centers. Its early-morning hours overlap with a number of Asian and Middle Eastern markets, and its afternoon hours overlap with the North American market.

The Forex market is a 24-hour market almost 6 days a week. The markets are closed for only a short period of time on the weekends. As some financial centers close, others open; so the foreign exchange market can be viewed in terms of following the sun around the earth.

Although there is some overnight trading of stocks, it's a limited market with a lot less liquidity or volume.

If you learn about major news that might impact a foreign currency in which you trade, you have 24-hour access to act on that news. But if you learn about something regarding a stock you hold after the closing bell, you probably won't find a way to trade it until the next business day. This greatly decreases the chances of market gaps in Forex trading that can be found with stock trading.

Although 24-hour access might sound like a great opportunity, it can also create a money-management nightmare. As a trader, you must realize that a sharp move in a foreign currency exchange rate can occur during any hour, at any place in the world. Large currency dealers use various techniques to monitor markets 24 hours a day, and many even keep their trading desks open on a 24-hour basis. Other financial institutions pass the torch from one geographic location to another rather than stay open around the clock.

The volume of currency traded does not flow evenly throughout the day. Over any 24-hour period, there are times of heavy activity and times when the activity is relatively light. Most trading takes place when the largest numbers of potential counterparties are available or accessible on a global basis.

Business is heaviest when both the U.S. markets and the major European markets are open. That is when it is morning in New York and afternoon in London. In the New York market, nearly two thirds of the day's trading activity takes place in the morning hours before the London markets close. Activity in the New York market slows in the mid to late afternoon after the European markets close and before the Asian markets of Tokyo, Hong Kong, and Singapore open.

Who Trades Foreign Currency?

Although everyone talks about how the world is becoming a "global village," the foreign exchange market comes closest to actually functioning as one.

So who is doing all this buying and selling? Only a limited number of major dealer institutions participate actively in foreign exchange. They trade with each other most often, but also trade with other customers. Most of these major players are commercial banks and investment banks. They're located in financial centers around the world, but are closely linked by telephone, computers, and other electronic means.

The central bank for most of these major dealer institutions is the Bank for International Settlements (BIS), which covers the foreign exchange activities for 2,000 dealer institutions around the world. The bulk of foreign exchange trades are actually handled by a much smaller group. BIS estimates that 100 to 200 market-making banks worldwide handle the bulk of all trades.

Many different types of institutions and individuals are involved in the foreign exchange trading world. These include commercial banks, governments, broker/dealers, corporations, investment-management firms, and speculators/individuals.

Commercial Banks

Commercial banks handle the vast amount of commercial foreign exchange trading through the interbank market. Most of this trading is done through efficient electronic systems.

Governments

Most governments around the world conduct their foreign exchange trading through their central banks. These central banks control the money supply, inflation, and/or interest rates for their respective countries. In most cases they also try to maintain target rates set for their currencies by the government decision makers. In the United States, the target exchange rates are set by the U.S. Treasury Department working with the Federal Reserve, which actually conducts all foreign currency exchange for the U.S. government.

Sometimes central banks act on behalf of the government to influence the value of the country's currency. For example, if the U.S. government believes the currency is weak, the Federal Reserve starts buying U.S. dollars and even encourages other friendly nations to do so to boost the value of the dollar. If the dollar is thought to be too strong, the Federal Reserve begins selling U.S. dollars on the foreign exchange market or encourages other countries to do so. Governments can also adapt new economic policies to affect the value of its country's currency.

Brokers or Dealers

Retail brokers or dealers act as intermediaries between the banks and individual traders. Individuals and companies who work through brokers or dealers do so because it gives them the ability to trade anonymously through an intermediary. Brokers or dealers also have much lower minimum trade size requirements than large banks, which allow individuals to access the market.

This retail foreign exchange market represents only about 2 percent of the total foreign exchange market. The volume of retail trades through dealers totals about $25 to $50 billion daily. All online trading of foreign exchange currency is done through retail dealers or brokers.

Most brokers do not provide individuals with direct access to the true interbank market because very few clearing banks are willing to process the relatively small orders placed by individuals.

Corporations

Corporations trade foreign currency primarily so that they can operate globally or invest internationally. For example, a U.S. manufacturer may buy parts from a manufacturer in Singapore. When it comes time to pay for those parts, the U.S. manufacturer will need to pay for them with Singapore dollars.

Investment-Management Firms

Investment-management firms, which manage large accounts for other entities, including pension funds and endowments, trade foreign currency for the portfolios they manage, which enables them to buy foreign securities, including stocks and bonds, for their clients' portfolios. In most cases, these transactions are secondary to the actual investment decision; in some cases, however, the investment-management firms do speculate for their clients with the goal of generating profits on the currencies traded while limiting risk. Most investment-management firms place their Forex transactions through a dealer. Speculators

All individuals who participate in the foreign currency market are considered speculators. Although you may hear controversy about the role of speculators in the foreign exchange market, they do provide an important function for the market. They provide a means for companies or people who don't want to bear the risk of foreign exchange trading to find an individual or institution that does want to take on that risk for the reward of future profits.

The largest speculators in the world of foreign exchange currency are hedge funds. These funds trade for a group of wealthy individuals and institutions that want them to use aggressive strategies in the hopes of reaping large profits.

Hedge funds can use strategies not permitted by mutual funds, including swaps and derivatives. Hedge funds are restricted by law to no more than 100 investors per fund, so minimum investment levels are high, ranging from $250,000 to more than $1 million per investor. Hedge fund managers not only collect a management fee for their work, they also all get a percentage of the profits, usually around 20 or 30 percent.

A Brief History

The foreign exchange market as we know it today is relatively new. It was started just a little more than 40 years ago, in 1973. But, of course, money has been around a lot longer than that. In this chapter, we review how money got started and how the current foreign exchange market developed.

Starting in Babylon

You must travel all the way back to the ancient kingdom of Hammurabi (third century B.C.E.) in Babylon to find the origins of banking. In those days, the royal palaces and temples served as secure places for the safe-keeping of grains and other commodities. People who deposited their commodities in the palaces and temples were given receipts that they could use to claim their commodities at a later date or give to others in payment for something else. These bills became the first known form of money.

Egypt also started a similar system of banking, providing state warehouses for the centralization of harvests. The written orders that depositors received were used to pay debts to others, including tax gatherers, priests, and traders.

Prior to these systems of deposits and receipts, the barter of goods was the primary way a person paid for things. Egypt moved from these paper notes to introduce the first coins. The earliest countable metallic money was made of bronze or copper from China. Other objects used for coins were spades, hoes, and knives, also known as tool currencies. The ancient Greeks during the time of Julius Caesar used iron nails as coins

When people engaged in foreign exchange, which was primarily in connection with military activities, the primary currencies used in trade were precious metals. Initially, precious metals were traded by weight, but a gradual transition was made from weight to quantity.

During the Middle Ages, the need for a currency other than coins or precious metals arose. Middle Eastern moneychangers were the first to use paper currency rather than coins for trade.

The dominant world currency before WWII was the British pound. The British pound lost its seat at the top of the currency world during WWII because Germany launched a massive counterfeiting campaign to destroy the power of the pound. All confidence in the pound was lost during WWII.

The U.S. dollar, which was in disgrace since the market crash of 1929, emerged from WWII as the currency of choice, which is still true today. The U.S. dollar remains the favored currency for most foreign exchanges. The U.S. economy boomed after WWII, and the United States emerged as a world economic power. The other big advantage of the United States was that it was one of few countries that hadn't felt the ravages of war on its own shores, so its massive infrastructure was still intact.

Bretton Woods Accord

After the war, the world's economy was in shatters. Something needed to be done to design a new global economic order and put all the pieces of the global economy back together. The United Nations Monetary Fund convened a global monetary and financial conference in Bretton Woods, New Hampshire, with representatives from the United States, Great Britain, and France, as well as 730 delegates from all 44 allied nations, to design a new global economic order.

The allies decided to hold the conference in the United States because it was the only place in the world not destroyed by war that was suitable for the conference. The conference ended with an accord, aptly named the Bretton Woods Accord.

The U.S. dollar emerged from Bretton Woods as the world's benchmark currency. One of the chief features of the new Bretton Woods system of foreign exchange was an obligation for each country to adopt a monetary policy that pegged the value of their currency to the U.S. dollar. The price of the US. dollar was pegged to gold at $35 per ounce, which became known as the gold standard.

Each country had to maintain its currency within a fixed value—plus or minus 1 percent —in terms of its peg to the U.S. dollar. This is known as a fixed exchange rate. The IMF was given the ability to bridge temporary imbalances of payments. The central bank of each country was required to intervene in the foreign exchange market if its country's exchange rate fluctuated more than 1 percent in either direction. The agreement initially served to bring stability to other countries and the global foreign exchange market. It succeeded in reestablishing stability in Europe and Japan. Until the 1970s, the Bretton Woods system helped to control economic conflict and achieve the goals set by the leading countries involved, especially the United States.

Initially this system worked well and helped to fuel the world's economic growth, but the system eventually fell under its own weight. As more and more countries converted their dollars to gold, the U.S. gold reserves dwindled. Pressures started to build on the gold peg, and an attempt to ease the problem started in 1968 when a new system called special drawing rights (SDR) was established. Dollar exchange between banks was done using SDRs and was managed by the International Monetary Fund. Countries were encouraged to hold dollars rather than convert those dollars to gold.

By 1971, the United States had enough gold to cover only about 22 percent of its reserve obligations. There was no way the United States could cover the paper dollars at the exchange rate of $35 per ounce of gold as set by the Bretton Woods Accord.

On August 15, 1971, President Nixon single-handedly closed the gold window and made the dollar inconvertible to gold directly, except on the open market—removing the U.S. need to balance the value of the dollar to the value of the gold held in its reserves. He made this decision without consulting with other members of the international monetary system and even without talking with the State Department.

Nixon's shocking move killed the Bretton Woods Accord and threw the entire world's monetary system into shock. After the shock wore off, the United States led the efforts to develop a new system of international monetary management. During the next several months, the United States held a series of multilateral and bilateral negotiations with other countries known as the Group of Ten to try to develop the new system. Participating countries were Belgium, Canada, France, Germany, Italy, the Netherlands, Sweden, Switzerland, the United Kingdom, and the United States. Today the Group of Ten still exists, but Japan has joined its ranks, bringing the total to 11 countries, although it is still called the Group of Ten.

Smithsonian Agreement

In December 1971, the Group of Ten met at the Smithsonian Institution in Washington, D.C., and created the Smithsonian Agreement, which devalued the dollar to $38 per ounce with trading allowed up to

2.25 percent above or below that value. Dollars could not be used to convert directly to gold. Instead, the Group of Ten officially adopted the SDR system, and the IMF held the responsibility of keeping the system in balance.

The United States continued its deficit spending, and the value of the U.S. dollar continued to fall. Gold's value began floating on the international markets, and its value gradually edged up to $44.20 per ounce in 1971 and $70.30 per ounce in 1972. Countries abandoned any peg to the U.S. dollar and let their currencies float. By 1976, all the developed countries' currencies were floating, and exchange rates were no longer the primary way governments administered monetary policy.

Today the currencies of developed countries float, but many of the emerging countries still peg the value of their currency to the U.S. dollar or to a basket of currencies from a number of countries.

European Monetary System

At about the same time as the Smithsonian Agreement, European countries established a European Joint Float. The nations that joined this system included West Germany, France, Italy, the Netherlands, Belgium, and Luxembourg. The basic system was close to the exchange rate regime established at Bretton Woods.

The European Joint Float failed at about the same time as the Smithsonian Agreement, but the decision among the Europeans to work together economically remained in place. The European countries began working together officially in 1957, long before the European Joint Float, under a treaty that formed the European Economic Community.

When the European Joint Float failed, the European nations worked together to form the European Monetary System (EMS) in 1979, which included most of the nations of the European Union. The goal of the EMS was to stabilize foreign exchange and counter inflation among the members of the EMS.

Periodic adjustments raised the values of the currencies whose economies were strong and lowered the values of the weaker ones. By 1986, a simpler system based on national interest rates was used to manage the currency values.

By the early 1990s, the EMS started to show strains, especially after Germany was reunited. Many European countries had very different economic policies, and faced varied economic conditions. Great Britain permanently withdrew from the EMS in 1991.

The EMS began efforts in the 1990s to establish a common currency in Europe. Its first step was to create the European Central Bank in 1994. By 1998, the bank was responsible for setting a single monetary policy and interest rate for the nations that chose to participate.

At the same time as the European countries moved to coordinate currency exchange, they also worked toward political and defense cooperation. The

European Union (EU) was formed in 1992 with the Treaty of Maastricht.

By 1998, the first members of the European Central Bank were Austria, Belgium, Finland, France, Germany, Ireland, Luxembourg, the Netherlands, Portugal, and Spain. All cut their interest rates to a nearly uniform low level with the hope that this would promote growth and prepare for the unified currency. In 1999, the unified currency, the euro, was adopted by these countries.

Euro coins and notes did not begin to circulate until January 2002. Within two months, local currencies were no longer accepted as legal tender within the countries that had adopted the euro.

Great Britain is not the only European nation that has decided not to adopt the euro. Denmark and Sweden also decided to maintain their currencies. Citizens of all three countries oppose the adoption of the euro.

None of the countries that joined the EU since the fall of the Soviet Union have adopted the euro either, but several are working to meet the economic requirements to do so. Countries must meet strict economic guidelines before becoming part of the EMS and adopting the euro. These requirements set limits on allowable government deficits and interest rates.

Today's Foreign Exchange Markets

Today's system of floating exchange rates is not a carefully planned system. Instead, it was one born by default as the Smithsonian Agreement and the European Joint Float failed to gain momentum. Yet the foreign exchange market is by far the largest and most liquid market in the world today.

The floating system allows the values of currencies to rise and fall based on the basic laws of supply and demand. When the supply of a particular currency is high, the price (relative exchange rate) of the currency begins to drop because there is more supply available than demand. The opposite is true when the supply of a currency is tight. When less money is available for trade, the price (relative exchange rate) of the currency goes up because more people want the currency than what is available for purchase.

Major currencies today move independently from other currencies. They can now be traded by anyone from individual retail investors to large central banks. Central banks do intervene occasionally to influence the exchange rate for their country's currency.

Forex & the Value of Information

When trading Forex, you need to know a lot more than just the exchange rate between the two currencies you want to trade. You also need to know about the economic and political conditions of the countries whose currencies you plan to trade. In addition, you want to watch for any dramatic moves in the value of either currency in the currency pair you plan to trade that might impact the value of that trade. You should also be aware of any upcoming economic announcements that could affect the volatility or the relative value of the currency you are considering trading, so that you can determine the best times to trade.

You might wonder whether currency trading is the best market for you to trade, or if some other market would be better for you, such as stocks or futures. This chapter examines the best places to get news about the currencies you are trading and compares Forex to other trading opportunities.

Getting the News About Money

When it comes to finding news about the financial markets, you may already be aware of the three top news sources:

• The Wall Street Journal (www.wsj.com) is the most respected daily business newspaper. You do need to buy a subscription to read the articles online but the expense is well worth it, no matter what type of trading you plan to do.

- Bloomberg (www.bloomberg.com) is the leading global provider of financial news. It does have a radio and a television station, which is great if your local cable provider includes it in your package; but if not, you can always access its information online.

- The Financial Times (www.ft.com), which is based in London, provides an excellent overview of the financial news from a European perspective. When trading foreign currency, it's critical to understand the news from a global perspective.

You should also read the key newspapers and financial websites for whichever country's currency you plan to trade.

Staying Alert to Breaking Currency News

Coverage of breaking news regarding currency and other financial issues is best found on one of the top two financial cable networks:

- Bloomberg Television is a 24-hour news channel that reports on key financial news.

- CNBC is a world leader for covering business news stories and broadcasts financial news highlights throughout the day. You can find more in-depth coverage of contemporary business issues during its evening programs.

Comparing Forex

You are probably asking, "Is trading Forex worth the risk?" and "How does it compare to other trading opportunities, such as futures and stocks?" or "Should I stick to a less-risky investment alternative?" The sections that follow discuss all these thoughts.

Forex vs. Futures

Forex gives the trader many advantages over trading futures. The biggest advantage Forex has is that you can trade the market 24 hours a day, and trading only briefly closes on the weekends. It is rare for you to face a period of illiquidity (not being able to trade) in the Forex market, whereas you are limited to the times the exchanges are open in the futures market.

If you hear news that could affect your positions at almost any time of day or night, you can trade on the Forex market, but you'll have to wait until the exchanges open on the futures market. This gives the Forex trader more flexibility and continuous market access, which just isn't available to the futures trader.

Foreign exchange is the principal market of the world. The monetary volume (US$2 trillion a day) and participation in the Forex market far exceeds any other financial market, including futures or stocks. Because the market is so large and available 24 hours a day, it is not affected by trading programs that can easily manipulate the stock or futures market.

If you study any market trading throughout the civilized world, you can quickly see that money is the root of all pricing. Global finance is distributed and redistributed using money through many different channels and different financial derivatives.

Forex is where the "big boys" trade—that's all the major banking institutions in the world—but Forex can also provide the small speculator with the opportunity for large profit potential, although the trader also has to be prepared for the corresponding large risk of trading foreign currency.

Another big advantage for Forex traders is that the fees are typically less than those found in the futures market. All traders, whether in futures or Forex, will find that financial instruments have a spread, which is the difference between the bid (the price at which a buyer will buy) and ask (the price at which a seller will sell) price. In the Forex market, you only have to worry about the spread; in the futures market, however, you often have to pay commission charges, as well as clearing and exchange fees, on top of the spread.

Better leverage is another advantage you can find when trading foreign currencies rather than futures. Trading using leverage is also called trading on margin. Spot currency traders have one low-margin requirement for trades conducted 24 hours a day. Futures traders can have one margin requirement for "day" trades and a different margin requirement for "overnight" positions.

Forex vs. Stocks

When trading Forex, you can primarily focus your attention on four major currency pairs (euro/U.S. dollar, U.S. dollar/yen, British pound/ U.S. Dollar, U.S. dollar/Swiss franc) with the potential to make a decent profit. These currency pairs are the most commonly traded, and the most liquid. You can add about 34 second-tier currencies for variation, but only if you commit yourself to the extra research time. With the majors, you can spend a lot less time on your computer researching potential trades and more time on other things you enjoy doing.

When you consider stocks, you have to choose among 8,000 stocks: 4,500 on the New York Stock Exchange and 3,500 on the NASDAQ. How do you pick the stocks you want to trade, and how do you make the time to continually research the companies you do pick?

Stocks are viewed by many as an investment vehicle, but in the past 15 years stocks have taken on a much more speculative role. Securities face more and more volatility every day, especially with the forces of day trading and other factors you can't predict.

How many times have you heard that a large mutual fund was buying a particular stock or basket of stocks and those trades created unexpected movement in a stock you held? Mutual funds can also influence the market at the end of the fiscal year, just to make the numbers look better on a financial report.

No matter what some firms may claim, the stock market can be moved by large fund buying and selling, and the movement can take place before you have time to react. It is not uncommon for a mutual fund to sell or buy a particular stock for a few days in a row.

Another big advantage spot currency trading offers to traders is that there is no middleman, so it costs less to trade. If you work directly with a dealer, who is a primary market-maker, you do not deal through a middleman. However, brokers operate through a bank or an FCM, so they may charge additional fees to cover the added costs.

In the stock market, you have centralized exchanges, which means you have middlemen who run those exchanges, and they need to be paid, too. The cost of these middlemen can be in both time to do the trade and money. Spot currency trading doesn't have any middlemen.

Analysts and brokerage firms are less likely to influence the Forex market than the stock market. Too many scandals have been exposed since 2000 that show how analysts told clients to buy a stock while calling it garbage (and worse) in e-mails behind the scenes. These analyst cheerleaders kept the Internet and technology moving upward, whereas stock investors unknowingly bought into companies that ultimately proved to be worthless.

The difference in trading foreign currency is that the primary market for the currency is driven by the world's largest banks and foreign governments. Analysts don't drive the flow of deals in the foreign currency market. All they can do is analyze the flow that is occurring.

If you trade in the stock market, you've probably found that there are different costs depending upon how you trade. You pay more fees if you call in your order or ask for specific types of orders, such as a stop or limit order to minimize your risk. You should not find additional costs when placing an order for trading in foreign currency.

Margins and leverage opportunities are much better in the Forex market, too. In spot trading, you can use your profits on open positions to add to those positions. That's something you might wish you could do when you own a hot stock and want to capitalize on the profits you've made by buying more of that stock. Although it's not possible in stock trading, you can do it when trading spot currency.

Forex vs. Other Less-Risky Investments

If you are concerned about the risks of Forex trading and prefer less-risky investments, such as bonds and mutual funds, Forex trading is probably not for you. If avoidance of risk is your primary investment concern, you probably won't be comfortable trading in the spot currency market.

Whether you are trading Forex, stock, or futures, you must be willing to take on risk and must understand that the money you use for trading could be lost. There is no insurance to protect your money (except occasionally offered on stock accounts), and you should only trade with money that you can afford to lose.

Changing Value As A Constant

Money makes the world go 'round, and lots of things can impact the value of that money. You can't control any of these factors that change the value of money, but you definitely need to understand what they are so that you can make tactical decisions about when to buy or sell a particular currency.

This chapter reviews the key factors that can impact the value of currencies, including basic economics, political change, interest rate changes, international investment patterns, inflation predictions, and money or tax policies adopted by governments and central banks.

Economics and Business Cycles

Currency, just like any other item that is bought or sold, can be impacted by the basics of economics and the business cycle. The laws of supply and demand are just as valid when talking about the value of currency as they are when talking about the value of any commodity.

When the supply of a particular currency is high, the price for that currency goes down as holders of the currency try to find ways to get rid of it. For example, if everyone decides that they don't want to hold U.S. dollars anymore and tries to sell them, to do so they would likely have to lower their price to find a buyer. In this case, there is more supply than demand.

You can compare this to the sale of real estate in your neighborhood. When there are a lot of houses on the market, they may sit unsold for many months. If someone must move because of a job change or some other reason, that person will likely price his or her home to sell (price it below what all other homes are listed for) to get it sold more quickly.

Conversely, when the supply of the currency is low and there are more people who want to buy it than there is currency available, the price of the currency goes up as buyers compete for the currency. In this case, there is more demand than there is supply. Using the same comparison, you can relate this to home sales in your neighborhood. When there are few homes available, buyers will offer the full asking price and sometimes bid that price even higher to be sure to get the home.

You may be wondering how a market could suddenly be flooded with a currency to increase supply and ultimately drive the price of the currency down. Well, that's one role governments and central banks take when they want to impact the value of a currency.

Governments can also decide they want the value of their currency to increase, and they have the buying power to buy currency and make the availability of their currency scarce. This will make the price of the currency rise.

Government manipulation is not the only thing that can impact the value of a currency economically. The action of businesses and consumers as a whole can drive currency values up and down. However, because the Forex market has so much volume, with more than US$2 trillion traded daily, it is highly unlikely that one single entity could impact the value of a currency for a significant period of time.

The good news for currency traders is that they have the potential to make money no matter what direction the market moves. Whether the business world is prospering and we're in the middle of a bull market (a market in which prices are rising and business is expanding) or we are experiencing a slowdown in the middle of a bear market (a market in which prices are dropping and business is contracting), it is still possible to make money during either condition by trading currencies.

The key is to know which kind of market each country is facing and how that market is impacting the value of the currency. Remember that each currency trade involves at least two countries: the country of the currency you are selling and the country of the currency you are buying.

Political Developments

Political changes can have the most dramatic effects on the value of a currency. They also can happen very quickly (such as a coup by the military). So when you choose the currencies you want to trade, be sure you understand the politics of the country for each currency you follow.

You may hear about some incredible opportunity for trading the currency of a developing country, but be very cautious with such rumors. The more unstable the country's politics, the greater the chance you will be burned in currency trading. Be very careful about trading on rumors, especially in developing markets.

Even in the most stable countries, after an election in which the party in power changes, the impact on the currency can be significant. For example, in the United States, if the current president and his party in power believe a strong dollar is good for the economy, the U.S. government can reduce the supply of its currency by buying up dollars and thus force the price to rise.

Conversely, if the party in power changes with the next election and the new president believes a weaker dollar will increase U.S. exports and decrease imports, the government could take moves to weaken the dollar (lower its price) by increasing its supply on the open market. So even in a very stable country, you may find that political change can impact the future value of a currency.

How the party in power manages the country's domestic economy can also be critical. When the economy is in a period of growth with relative price stability, the currency of that country will be in demand. Although if a country is facing political turmoil, high inflation, or has few marketable exports, its currency will be less attractive.

Changes in Interest Rates

When interest rates go up or down, the value of a currency can fluctuate. When interest rates go up, the currency is more attractive to currency investors because they'll make more money holding it. So when interest rates rise, more traders and investors buy that currency, the supply of the currency becomes scarce, and the price of the currency rises.

The opposite happens when interest rates go down. Fewer investors want to hold on to the currency, especially if they can find a better deal someplace else. Many traders and investors start to sell the currency, and its supply goes up. As supply increases and demand decreases, the value of the currency goes down.

Be sure to watch the interest rate fluctuations in each of the countries whose currency you trade. Follow the pronouncements of the central banks and governments about their plans to raise or lower interest rates. Markets move rapidly on this type of news, and you can quickly get caught on the losing side if you hold a currency whose price is dropping because interest rates have just been lowered.

International Stock News

News about the stock market can also drive currency values up or down. Although the major stock markets (such as NASDAQ, New York Stock Exchange, American Stock Exchange, London Stock Exchange, and Tokyo Stock Exchange) get the most coverage, you'll find there are stock exchanges and stock news to be had in most developed countries and many developing countries.

When trading foreign currency, you need to keep your eye on the international stock market news, not only news from the U.S. exchanges. Keep an eye on stock index movements in any of the countries whose currency you trade. Stock market moves can impact the value of a currency.

Inflationary Expectations

Inflation and its impact on the economy can significantly impact the value of the currency, too, so you need to keep your eyes and ears open for news about any inflationary expectations within the countries you monitor.

Of course, one of the first things to be changed if the central bank or government believes inflation may be on the rise is the interest rates. Remember that interest rate fluctuations can have a major impact on the supply and demand for the currency and ultimately the price at which the currency will sell.

Currency of countries that are not raising their interest rates during an inflationary period will likely decrease in price, whereas the price of currency in countries that are increasing the interest rates will likely increase.

Inflation can also impact where imports and exports are bought and sold as prices rise or fall. This will change a country's balance of payments and ultimately impact the value of the country's currency.

The payments and liabilities (debt) owed to foreign countries are listed as debits. The payments and obligations due from other countries are listed as credits. When that balance of payments is out of whack, especially if the country owes more than it receives, the value of the currency can drop.

The United States does have one huge advantage that enables it to run large trade deficits: the U.S. dollar is the primary currency for all oil trades with OPEC. Every country that wants to buy oil from an OPEC country must use U.S. dollars to buy oil. Some call these dollars petrodollars. That helps to prop up the value of the U.S. dollar.

Inflation occurs when too much money is available. The value of the money will decline and prices in the country will rise as exports become more expensive. When too little money is available, the economy will become sluggish, and unemployment will rise.

International Investment Patterns

Money (and currency buyers) flows to the currency where traders or investors can get the highest return with the least amount of risk. Investors flock to a country when stocks and bonds command a high rate of return with relatively low risk.

For buyers to buy those stocks and bonds, they first must buy the currency. That increases the demand for the currency, and the currency's price increases.

When you're trading foreign currency, don't only look at the charts of the currency moving up and down. You also want to follow news of what investors in other types of financial markets are doing.

You can get many clues by watching the flow of international investments. Read the key financial news sites, such as The Wall Street Journal (www.wsj.com), Bloomberg (www. bloomberg.com), Business Week (www.businessweek.com), and CNN (www.cnn.com) to find information about investment waves to locate your next trading opportunity.

Policies Adopted by Governments and Central Banks

Governments and central banks can impact a currency's value using two key tools: foreign exchange rates and tax policy. Government officials closely monitor economic activity to keep the money supply at a level appropriate to achieve their economic goals. Money supply can be increased or decreased, which is usually done by changing the interest rate or manipulating the supply of money on the market.

In the United States, the government agency responsible for setting foreign exchange rates is the U.S. Treasury Department. The entity responsible for carrying out those decisions is the New York Federal Reserve Bank under the direction of the Federal Open Market Committee (FOMC) of the Federal Reserve.

The U.S. Treasury can impact exchange rates. If the U.S. government believes the

exchange rate does not reflect fundamental economic conditions, it can instruct the New York Fed to buy or sell currency in the foreign exchange market to impact the value of the U.S. dollar. Sometimes the United States works diplomatically with other countries to get them to intervene, too, by buying or selling U.S. dollars.

The New York Federal Reserve also acts as an agent on behalf of other countries' central banks and international organizations. When the New York Fed acts as an agent for another country or organization, these transactions do not necessarily reflect the policy of the U.S. government. These actions can be done openly through the Forex market, or they can be done discreetly through a confidential dealer in the brokers' market.

Tax policy can also significantly affect the value of a country's currency. Tax policies can encourage or discourage investment by domestic businesses as well as by foreign investors.

How Traders Can Take Advantage of These Changes

Savvy traders learn to keep their eyes on all these factors as they look for opportunities to make money by trading currency. Key events to watch for include the following:

• News of political instability around the world drives up the value of currency from stable countries, such as the U.S. dollar, Japanese yen, Swiss franc, British pound, or the euro, as people seek safe havens in stable countries.

• A country's currency value can increase as foreign investors seek better interest rates in countries with more attractive interest rates than they can find in their own country. Watch interest rates move as you look for trading opportunities.

•   The currency of a developing country that is making successful economic moves usually experiences an increase in that country's currency as foreign investors seek new investment opportunities. As you become a more experienced Forex trader, watch for an increase of investment dollars into a developing country; the currency may also increase in value.

Currency traders try to predict the behavior of other market participants. If they correctly anticipate the strategies of others, they can act first and beat the crowd. You basically have two possible currency strategies: buy currency at a low price hoping to sell it later at a higher price, or sell currency at a high price hoping to buy it back later at a lower price.

In trying to predict their best moves, currency traders who use fundamentals try to determine whether the current price of a currency reflects the true economic conditions in the country. They look at inflation, interest rates, and the relative strength of the economy to make a determination about the future value of the country's currency. If they believe the currency is undervalued, they buy it with the expectations that the currency's value will increase. If they believe the currency is overvalued and they own some of it, they dump it.

Forex Trading 101

The Forex market is the center of world capital, over which lies the interconnection and movement of each country's capital and investment funds. For instance, an Asian speculative fund investing in Austria's Treasury bonds, or a Japanese financial company devoting some of its assets to the Argentina stock exchange, each of these international transactions is made possible through the Forex market.

The Forex market is open round the clock, six days a week. It enables Forex traders to trade positions at whatever time they please or act on events and news, as they happen. In this market, large funded trades as high as a billion dollars can be transacted in a matter of seconds. The average daily Forex trading volume is about 15 times the size of the world's equity markets. Hence, the Forex market is basically a trader's market.

The large part of currency trading volume is based on speculation, as opposed to commercial and financial transactions. Speculation means that Forex traders buy and sell foreign exchange positions for short term profits based on a day to day, hour to hour, or minute to minute fluctuation of prices.

The biggest contributor of currency trading volume, as much as 75 %, is the major currencies. The major currencies represent the wealthiest and most developed economies.

You might ask, what is the factor that contributes to the efficiency and ease of buying and selling securities, stocks, financial instruments, and assets such as Forex? That factor is liquidity. This refers to the overall level of market interest, or the level of buying and selling volume in the market at any point of time for a particular security, stock, financial instrument or asset. Simply put, the higher the level of liquidity, the deeper the market. The deeper the market, the level of efficiency and ease of buying and selling becomes higher.

Liquidity is an important factor since it measures how fast prices move between trade transactions over time. A highly liquid market can determine large trading volume transacted with minor changes in the price. Conversely, an illiquid market determines the prices as they move rapidly on lower trading volumes.

Depending on the time zone, global financial centers such as London, Sydney and Tokyo are open at any given time. Moreover, currency or Forex trading doesn't even halt its

operations for holidays. This means that the Forex market is open and active 24 hours a day, 7 days a week.

With respect to Forex trading in the Asia Pacific Region, the financial trading centers are Singapore, Hong Kong, Sydney and Tokyo. It is important to note that most of the transactions in this region are focused on the Japanese Yen currency pairs.

With respect to Forex trading in the European Region, it is important to note that most of the transactions in this area are focused on the European currencies and the Euro cross-currency pairs.

With respect to Forex trading in the North American Region, it is important to note that on most days, market interest rates and market liquidity decrease significantly in New York during afternoons. On relatively less active trading days, the lower market interest results in stagnant prices. But on relatively more active trading days, the lower level of liquidity can trigger price movements. Traders also need to consider that lower levels of liquidity tend to prevail.

First and foremost, always remember that the various financial markets are markets of their own. This means that they function in accordance with their internal dynamics, which is based on empirical date, positions of large financial institutions, global news and general market sentiment. However, markets sometimes display degrees of correlation with each other. Hence, it is imperative for a Forex trader to consider each market as one unique market, a market of its own kind, and to trade between them individually.

The relationship of Forex with gold over the long term is mostly inverse, with a weaker currency most likely resulting to a higher price of gold, and a stronger currency most likely resulting to a lower price of gold. However, in the short term, each market has its own movements, fluctuations, dynamics and liquidity.

The relationship of Forex with oil is in conformity with the overall economic conditions of a financial district. For example, a high price of oil results to higher levels of inflation. And the higher the levels of inflation, the slower the economy's growth prospects. Conversely, a low price of oil results to lower levels of inflation. And the lower the levels of inflation, the faster the economy's growth prospects.

The Forex markets and the equity markets only occasionally intersect so there is not much empirical evidence that can lead to a correlation between the two financial markets. One example of the two financial markets intersecting is when a stock market reaches extraordinary levels of volatility and fluctuations, the currency experiences more pressure.

The relationship of Forex with bonds is intuitive because these two are both affected by expectations of interest rates by the stakeholders. There are times, however that the reaction of the Forex market moves faster compared to that of bonds. At other times, the reverse happens. That is, the reaction of bonds moves faster than that of the Forex market. As currency traders, you need to always be aware of the yield levels of the government bonds of the major currency countries. The purpose of this is to make sure that the expectations of the interest rate market are properly determined by the currency trader himself since changes in interest rates influence Forex markets.

Terms

There are essentially two types of trades you can make, depending on what you feel the market is going to do next: you can take a long position or a short position.

• Long Positions are opened when you buy under the assumption the currency will increase in value. In other words, you're looking to buy it low and sell it high for a profit.

• Short Positions are opened by borrowing the currency from the broker when you feel the market will decrease in value. When you borrow from the broker you must return what you borrowed by buying it back. If the currency decreased in value, then you buy it for less than it was borrowed for, making a profit in the process.

In a bullish market prices are rising. In a bearish market prices are dropping.

In the Forex market currencies are traded in pairs, so each trade is long for one currency and short for the other. If you expect the US dollar to be long, you would expect the other currency in the pair to be short. If that's unclear don't worry, we cover this in more detail later.

When you buy or sell currency the order must be filled, meaning when you sell 500 shares someone is buying, and when you buy 500 shares it means someone is selling. The broker you are working with has an order book, which is a list of buy and sell orders. This is electronic and is used to match orders quickly, to the point of being immediate in most cases.

An order to buy is called bid and an order to sell is called ask. There is something called a bid/ask spread, which is the difference in price between the highest bid and the lowest ask in the order book.

Currency pairs are values that tell you the amount required to buy one unit. The first quotation is called a base and is the relative value of a currency unit against the unit of the other currency called a quote.

For example, the euro against the US dollar would look like EUR/USD 1.30, which means that one euro is exchanged for 1.30 US dollars.

Base/quote lets you know how much quote currency is required to buy one unit of the base currency.

The most commonly traded currency pairs are called the Majors which involve the following:

- Euro

- U.S. dollar

- Japanese yen

- Pound sterling

- Australian dollar

- Canadian dollar

- Swiss franc

The four most popular pairs are:

EUR/USD (euro/U.S. dollar)

USD/JPY (U.S. dollar/Japanese yen)

GBP/USD (British pound/U.S. dollar)

USD/CHF (U.S. dollar/Swiss franc)

The next three are also popular, just not as popular as the top four:

AUD/USD (Australian dollar/U.S. dollar)

USD/CAD (U.S. dollar/Canadian dollar)

NZD/USD (New Zealand dollar/U.S. dollar)

95% of all trading in Forex is a combination of these pairs, making the Forex market far more focused than other markets, like the stock market.

The major currency pairs all have USD in them, however, you can get a cross currency quote, as well. Common cross currency pairs are:

EUR/CHF

EUR/GBP

EUR/JPY

Some retail brokers trade in exotic currencies you don't normally find, such as Czech koruna, so if you are looking to trade something that's not in the "Majors" then you will need to shop around to find what you want.

The Forex comes in three delicious flavors: spot, forwards, and futures (probably the worst names for flavors I've ever heard).

The spot market is the largest Forex market. In fact, when people say "Forex" they mean the spot market. This is the market where currencies are bought and sold and the information is all current in real time.

The forward and future markets are based on the spot market. However, these markets are set for some future date. In the forward market, contracts are bought and are between two parties who have agreements set between them. In the futures market, contracts are bought and sold on an exchange like the Chicago Mercantile Exchange.

With currency futures, price is determined when the contract is signed and the pair is exchanged on a date in the future. With the spot Forex, the price is determined at the point of trade and the physical exchange takes place at the point of trade. Contracts in futures can be sold before the date of settlement. When we discuss strategies these come into play a little more, but most strategies discussed in this book focus on the spot Forex.

Even though you are buying another country's currency, you aren't really buying anything physical, like cash or coins. Think of buying foreign currency as buying shares in another country. You are betting on the country's economy, essentially.

You will likely trade in the spot Forex, but can trade in these other markets as well. But, these markets are typically used with large purchases between companies. For example, company XYZ Co. in the U.S. is making a large part for a European company that will cost 100 million euros to produce over the next 5 years. In order to hold the value of that 100 million Euros, XYZ Co. could use the future or forward market to lock in value. If the euro loses value in the next five years, it could throw off the sale otherwise.

Getting Started

By converting your money into a different currency, you hope that the other currency increases in value. When you convert it back to your original currency, you hope to make a profit.

For example, let's say you exchange $1000 U.S. dollars for $1100 Canadian dollars. The CAD/USD exchange rate goes up by .10, meaning the Canadian dollar has increased in value when compared to the U.S. dollar. You could exchange the $1100 Canadian dollars you have back to the U.S. dollar and get $1100 U.S. dollars, making a $100 USD profit.

A Forex quote will have a bid price and an ask price for a currency pair, which are quoted in relation to the base currency. When selling the base currency, the bid price is the price the broker is willing to pay to buy the base currency from you. In other words, it's the price you'll receive if you sell.

When buying the base currency, the ask price is what the broker is willing to sell you the base currency for in exchange for the quote currency. Let's take a look at an example:

Here is a typical currency quote: USD/CAD 1.2050/05. You would read that as bid = 1.2050 and the ask = 1.2055. Another way of looking at it is USD/CAD Bid/Ask. You could enter the position at 1.2055 or sell your position for 1.2050. The bid/ask spread of 0.0005 is a fee the broker takes.

This is where pips come in. No, not pips from a watermelon. A pip, also called a point, is the incremental change in a Forex price. A $1.50 in a Forex price would look like $1.5000. So going up one pip would look like going from $1.5000 to $1.5001. Pips aren't much, which is why there is so much leverage or money needed to make a profit. Leverage allows you to increase your buying power by ratios of 100:1 or even 200:1 and up.

You buy currencies in lots. A standard "lot" is $100,000. Don't get scared of that number since it will be made up of leverage. You can also do smaller lots like $10,000, called a mini-lot. Another high, scary number I know, but a mini-lot can be bought with $50 before leverage to give you a better feel for these high numbers.

You can get two different quotes for a currency pair. The first is directly, which is a simple foreign exchange quote where the foreign currency is the base. The second is the indirect quote, which is a currency pair which has the domestic currency as the base. So, if you're in Canada you can get a direct quote that would look like C$1.10 pre US $1. An indirect quote would look like C$1 = US$0.90.

The Forex market offers so much opportunity to make a profit, both in rising and declining markets alike. Every trade is done in a pair, so you are buying and selling at the same time: you're going long with one currency and short in another. In the stock market, in order to short a stock you need to wait for the uptick to enter, but since there are no "rules" in the Forex you can enter a short position any time you want.

Order Terms and Types:

•   Entry Order is an order that will execute your trade once the currency pair reaches a target price that you specified.

•   Stop Order is an order that becomes a market order once the price you set is reached.

•   Limit Order is an order to buy or sell the currency at a specific limit. The order will only be filled if the market trades at the price set or better.

•   GFD stands for "good for the day." It's an order that stays open until the day ends, which can be different depending on the broker since it's a 24-hour day, 5 days a week. So make sure you know what time that is for your broker.

•   GTC stands for "good until cancelled" which is an order that will remain active until you cancel it.

- OCO stands for "order cancels other." The order is placed below and above the current market price and if one of the orders is executed, the other one is cancelled. For example, a currency pair is at 1.2005. An OCO order could have an order to buy at 1.2010 in anticipation of a breakout. At the same time, the order could tell the broker to sell at 1.2000 if the price falls to that point. If you already hold a position in the currency pair, you will buy more if the price hits 1.2010, and if the price drops to 1.2000, you will sell. That way, if the breakout occurs the trader buys more and if the breakout doesn't happen, the order to sell is taken.

Leverage

In order to make profits off the small changes in the currency market, you need leverage. Leverage can work in different ways depending on your broker, but normally a currency trading account would see ratios of 50:1,100:1, 200:1 and up. You can put $50 of your money on a trade and leverage it to $10,000. For example, when a currency goes up a penny with $50 in, you make .50 cents. With $10,000 in you make $100. A penny is 100 pips. So if the currency pair changes by only 20 pips, you would need a lot more leverage to make that $100 in profits.

Think of leverage as a loan provided by the broker to you, the investor. The great thing about leverage is that to trade in amounts like $100,000 you only need to open your account with $1,000. This is because Forex brokers provide such low margin requirements. Margin borrowed money normally requires a large amount of capital to open an account in other markets, like stocks. For example, a day trader wanting to use leverage in the stock market must normally maintain a $25,000 account.

Your rewards potential is much higher and so is your risk. When you trade with borrowed money, keep in mind the broker has the right to sell at their discretion. If your position takes a big enough dive, the broker can decide to cut losses and sell. Every broker that you borrow from has this right, but many brokers won't make a move like that. Just be aware that all brokers can and some brokers do.

Margin-based leverage is determined by dividing the total transaction by the level of margin you are given. Check with your broker, but let's say you are required to deposit 1% of a total transaction amount as margin when trading one standard lot, which is $100,000. So your margin requirement is $1,000 or 100:1.

Protecting Your Trades

Risks are very real and scary in the Forex. This section will cover the things you should do to protect yourself. The good news is that when you have $200,000 on a currency pair, prices usually change by less than one cent in an entire day. It's not like putting $200,000 in a stock and watching it plummet, which is why with trading stocks you're only going to get leverage around 2:1.

The small movements of currency can be blinding to risks. Working with pips can throw a new trader off. Therefore, let's put this in real terms to get a feel for it. If you put $1,000 on a stock trade and the stock drops 1% you just lost $10. If you put $1,000 on a currency trade and took leverage at 100:1 and lost 1%, you just lost your $1,000. This is why so many new currency traders lose their account the day they open it.

When I say "usually" changes less than one cent, I don't mean "always," and even the small changes in pips that occur can hurt your account with such high leverage. Currencies aren't likely to drop like a stock, but their small movements happen fast.

Even with small pip movements you still have major risks. There are several methods currency traders use to limit and control their risk. Nothing is ever foolproof, but this system will help you minimize losses.

Never trade what you need to live on. Think of trading money as fun money or investment money you can afford to lose. Even with leverage trades, have a cushion and place stop losses where you need to. A stop is an order to buy or sell the trade at a price. So, if you enter the price at $1.2045, you would want to put a stop below your entry to cut your losses if the price falls below a certain point. Depending on the price action, you may decide that putting a stop loss 10 pips below your entry at $1.2035 would be best.

There is a common saying to "never let a winner turn into a loser," which is another way of reminding you to protect those profits! This is especially true in the Forex where you are using high leverage and fast moving pips. It's just poor money management otherwise. I suggest that all new Forex traders bank every 15 to 20 pips. You're making low profits, but your risk is low, too.

Stop losses: One of the better ways to do a stop loss, especially as a new trader, is to use a trailing stop. A trailing stop is about setting a near term target. If you want to scalp (take quick profits) those 15 pips, then when you reach 15, move your stop loss up to that point to lock in profits. Or, you can set a trailing stop that moves with your trade.

You can set a trailing stop for 5 pips, and as the trade moves up, the trailing stop does as well. Let's say you buy a currency pair at 1.2000 and set a trailing stop at

5 pips. If the price falls to 1.1995 the trade will sell. Let's say the price went from 1.2000 to 1.2050. Your trailing stop would be right behind you and be set at 1.2045. If the price went from 1.250 to 1.2047 the trailing stop stays at 1.2045, and won't sell until triggered. A trailing stop will likely kick you out early, cutting the chances of making additional profits, but it's recommended to new traders to help control risks. As you become better at reading information and charts and get a feel for price action, a trailing stop might not be the best choice.

Another popular tip is to never risk more than 2%. Let's look at an actual loss and the real effect it has. Let's say you start trading with $5,000. You lose 50% of your bank, o r$2,500. It now takes a 100% gain just to break even. A loss can dig you pretty deep, really fast. For new Forex traders, it's not uncommon to get hit with a loss of 75% of your bank, which would require a 400% gain to break even.

That's where the 2% rule comes in. You would have to lose 10 trades in a row to lose 20% of your bank. Make sure your stop loss is no more than 2% of your risk.

When you trade currency pairs, match up a strong with a weak. Every trade is for a long and a short. The good news in the Forex is that countries' economic outlooks don't change very fast. A strong currency may get an increased interest rate, which will increase your yield.

Never make a bad position worse. If you placed your stop loss, you did the right thing. However, traders without a stop loss on a sinking ship have a tendency to keep adding to their position, thinking they are getting a better price to buy and the trend will change. It may and it may not. However, you're gambling on a losing direction. It's almost always best to cut losses and move on.

In a market mostly out of your control, you need to make it a point to control the limited things you can. You control where you're entering a position. Your risk can be predetermined by entering a stop loss. Profit is unpredictable, but never let your loss be unpredictable.

Choosing a Broker

When you look for an online broker for stocks, the big factors are commissions and fees.

Since the currency brokers won't have commissions, you need to look for low spreads.

The spread is the difference between the price at which the currency can be purchased and the price at which it can be sold. Just like stock brokers can charge anywhere from $4.75 to $20 on trades, the difference in spreads for Forex brokers can be just as large. Shop around. If you plan to use the day trading strategies or even the swing trading strategies discussed later in this book, picking a low spread is especially important.

Your broker needs to offer real-time charts and tools to help you analyze the charts. The trading platform needs to offer what you're looking for and be easy to use.

Most brokers will offer different types of accounts, depending on the amount of capital you can bring to the table. Smaller accounts will be around $200 to

$300, while medium accounts around $2000 to $5000. The larger accounts can range from $10,000 and up.

Your job is to ensure that whatever your price point is for an account, you're getting the right tools.

Where is the Forex broker incorporated? Try to get one in the country you live in, or going with a US or UK broker works.

And last but not least, make sure they have 24-hour telephone support, especially if you are looking to trade at odd hours. There's nothing worse than losing power or internet in the middle of a big trade.

Types of Accounts

Once you pick a broker, it's time to find the account that fits you. There are three types of accounts...well four if you count micro accounts.

- **The Micro Account**

This lets you trade in $1,000 increments. You can open them for $25. They are used mainly for investors. Profits are...just not really there. Many new traders open a micro account for practice, but I recommend that you open a demo account (discussed later) for practice.

- **The Mini Account**

This account allows you to make trades in small lots. These accounts are great for people new to trading currencies. There is low risk in a mini account, but also low profits. You trade in $10,000 increments. It depends on your broker, but a mini account can be opened with anywhere from $250 to $500 and offers leverage as high as 400:1.

- **The Standard Account**

This is the most common type of account, which costs about $1,000 to open and trades in increments of $100,000. Some brokers want more then $1,000 to open and may request as much as $10,000 to open.

- **The Managed Trading Account**

These accounts are when the capital in them belongs to the investor, but the decisions are made by professionals. There are account managers who handle the account. There are two types of accounts under a managed trading account. The pooled fund account is when your money is put into a mutual fund with others' cash and the profits are shared with everyone. They are divided by the amount you contribute.

The other type of account is the individual account. The broker handles the account and makes decisions individually for each account.

Both of these accounts are great choices for people who want to get into the Forex market but don't want to manage their accounts. You can open one for as little as $2,000 for a pooled account and $10,000 for an individual account.

The downside is that there are commissions, which can be calculated monthly or annually, depending on the broker.

Choosing between Technical and Fundamental Analysis

What is Fundamental Analysis?

Fundamentals are the economic fundamentals of a security or asset (country in the case of Forex, stock in the case of the equity market) that are derived from the study of the news and information that reflect the macroeconomic and political situations of the country whose currencies and money are being traded. The process of deriving the fundamentals from the news and information gathered is called fundamental analysis. Fundamentals of a country are usually on the levels of interest rates, the monetary policy of the country's government and central bank, economic data reports by the national economic authority of the country, international trade flows, and international investment flows.

What is Technical Analysis?

Technical analysis is a form of market analysis that more often than not includes charting analysis, mathematical and empirical studies of price sensitivity and behaviors, trend line analysis, and momentum or moving averages. Technical analysis can provide the trader some guidelines regarding how the prices of currency move, allowing him to predict the future direction of price changes.

Rather than choosing to use fundamental or technical analysis, it would be beneficial for a Forex market trader, especially the new ones, to follow an approach that reconciles or combines the two. This will improve the Forex market trader's chances of spotting trade opportunities and handling Forex markets that are reacting to both fundamental and technical developments.

Every culture has its own jargon and slang. Most of these are self-explanatory, but it helps to ensure you know them.

- Cable - GBP (British Pounds)

- Sterling - GBP

- Pound - GBP

- Greenback - US dollar

- Buck - US dollar

- Swissie - Swiss franc

- Aussie - Australian dollar

- Kiwi - New Zealand dollar

- Loonie - Canadian dollar

- The little dollar - Canadian dollar

- Figure - Round number for currency like 1.4000

- Yard - A billion units

Economic Indicators

In stocks, it's hard but doable to assess a company, where they are and where they plan to be. However, in currencies you're basically buying a share in the country's economy. There are infinite variables that come into play. Here is a list of top sources of news and reports that move markets.

• World Banks are great ways to stay on top of interest rates and the economics of a country. It's not unheard of in other countries to have leaked reports come out before the official release date. There is no such thing as insider trading in the Forex market, so have at it. Of course, you run the risk of the report changing or being false, too. Check the websites of the different world banks to get these reports.

•   The Non-farm Payrolls are reported by the U.S. Bureau of Labor Statistics and show the total number of U.S. workers other than the workers in farms, government and a few other industries. Think of this number as representing 80% of the workers in the United States. This is a report that comes out monthly on the first Friday of every month. The Federal Reserve watches this report like a hawk with an eagle strapped to its back. Great visual. The report acts like a mini-census. Most companies will increase the hours worked before hiring new employees as a way of testing the demand for growth, which the report picks up on, too.

•   Retail Sales is a measure of the sale of retail goods over a time period. This is a monthly indicator that is released by the Census Bureau and the Department of Commerce, released two weeks after the month ends. These reports are used to compare to last year and previous years, not so much compared to last month. Retail is prone to seasonality, which means some things are bought in summer and others in winter. The month of December should be compared to other Decembers and not November.

• Durable Goods is released by the Bureau of Census and shows new orders placed with domestic companies for durable goods. These reports arrive twice a month. The durable goods report is a great way to get a feel for economic growth. Lots of orders placed to factories mean lots of work for the next few months (depending on the type of work).

• Purchasing Managers Index (PMI) is the measure of economic health of a specific sector. A PMI of more than 50 represents expansion of the sector. Under 50, and it's a decline. Keep in mind this index can be called the ISM index (Institute of Supply Management), as well.

• Consumer Price Index (CPI) is used to measure inflation or deflation. A large rise in the CPI during a short period can show a period of inflation, while a large drop in CPI in a short period can mark deflation.

• Jobless Claim Report comes out weekly every Thursday at 8:30am EST. The report shows the first-time filing for state unemployment in the United States. Take into account seasonality, since some jobs are more popular depending on the time of year. Think holidays, construction and outside work. This report comes out frequently, giving a up-to-date account of the economy. The less unemployed the better the economy, the more unemployed the worse.

• The Employment Situation Report or labor report comes out the first Friday of the month at 8:30am EST, released by the United States Bureau of Labor Statistics (BLS). There are actually two reports in one. The "establishment survey" is a sampling from over 400,000 business and is regarded as the most comprehensive labor report available. It includes hours worked and hourly earnings. The other report is the "household survey," which collects statistics from 60,000 households and estimates the total number of people out of work.

• Gross domestic product (GDP) is a broad measure of the country's economic performance. It's a measure of the total value of all finished goods and services produced in the country in a given year. There are two reports that come out before the final one, called the "advanced GDP report" and the "preliminary report." These hold more weight than the final report for traders, since the final report is considered a lagging indicator because it's news that already supports where the market is trending.

• Industrial Production Report is released monthly by the Federal Reserve. This report covers production in factories, mines and utilities in the United States. The number to watch is the capacity utilization ratio. When the number is between 80-

85% it's considered "tight," and shows that prices are likely to increase and supply may decrease. Below 80% is considered a decline in the economy and risk of recession.

All of these reports are must haves to gather information on currencies. These top reports can help you better understand the market and changes that occur. Economic indicators are any reports that detail a country's economic performance. Governments that trade currencies will have periodically published reports. The best places to find information are the websites of the governments and central banks of the currencies you are trading in. In some cases, the government is the bank, but both should have online information.

Candlesticks and Charts

This section will give you the basics for reading candlestick charts as well as technical data and trends. Your Forex broker will provide the charts and software. They are also available from both free and paid services online.

A candlestick chart is made up of images like the ones below. They can be green/white/empty or red/black/filled. A bullish candlestick has a price that closes higher than it opens. A bearish candlestick has a price that closes lower than it opens.

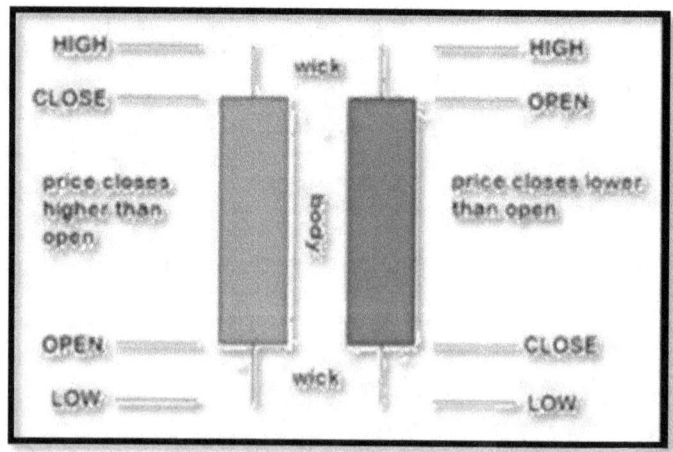

As you can see, candlesticks provide a lot of information with a quick glance. You can customize your screen to make candlesticks look a number of different ways.

Engulfing Candlestick patterns are formed when a small candle is followed by a large candle that eclipses the previous. For a bullish candlestick, that means a small black candlestick followed by a large white candlestick. For a bearish engulfing pattern, look for a small white candlestick followed by an engulfing black candlestick.

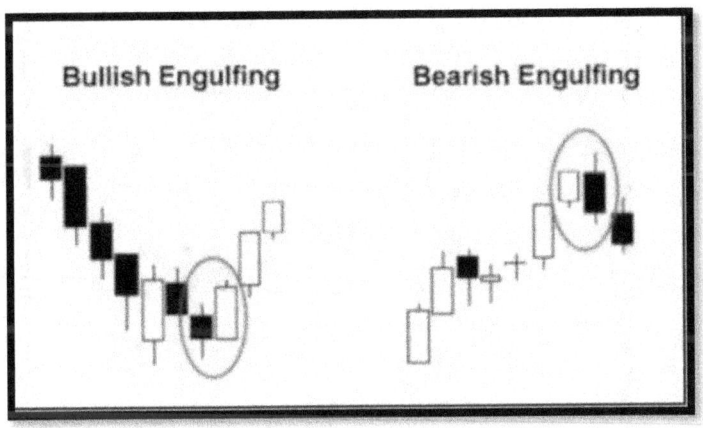

Inverted Hammer and Shooting Star: The inverted hammer is a pattern found after a downtrend and is a signal of reversal. The candle has a small lower body and a long upper wick which is at least two times as large as the short lower body. There should be little to no lower wick. The inverted hammer would have a white body, making it a bullish signal (uptrend). It's common to wait for another bullish candle to confirm the trend.

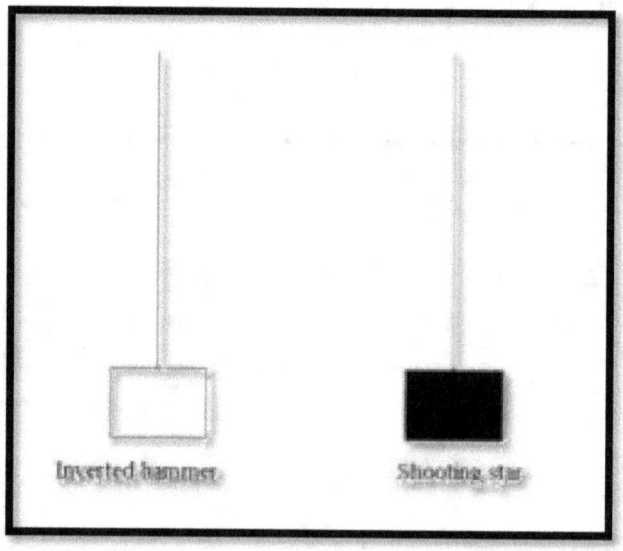

Inverted hammer   Shooting star

A shooting star is the same formation as an inverted hammer, but is bearish, appearing after an uptrend and is a signal of reversal having a black body.

The Hammer and the Hanging Man represent changes in the direction of trend. The hammer comes into formation after a downtrend with a white candlestick and the hanging man after an uptrend with a black candlestick.

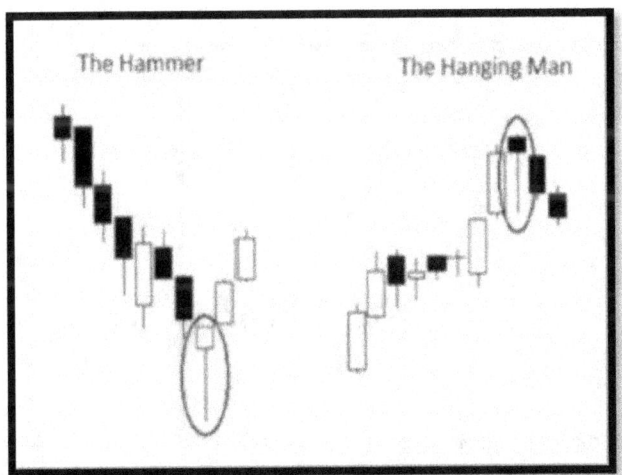

Harami candlestick patterns are when a large candlestick is followed by a smaller candlestick, with the body located within the range of the larger previous body. The bullish harami is in a downtrend of black candlesticks, while the harami pattern is a small white candlestick giving the signal of a reversal. The bearish version is a large white candlestick engulfing a small black candlestick after an uptrend signaling a reversal.

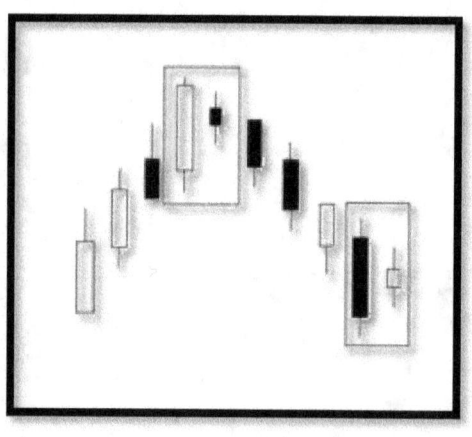

Dark Cloud Cover and Piercing Line: A dark cloud cover is when a black candlestick follows a long white candlestick and can signal a bearish trend. The black candlestick comes in higher than the previous white candlestick. It must have a closing price that is within the price range of the previous candlestick, but be below the midpoint between the open and closing prices of the previous day.

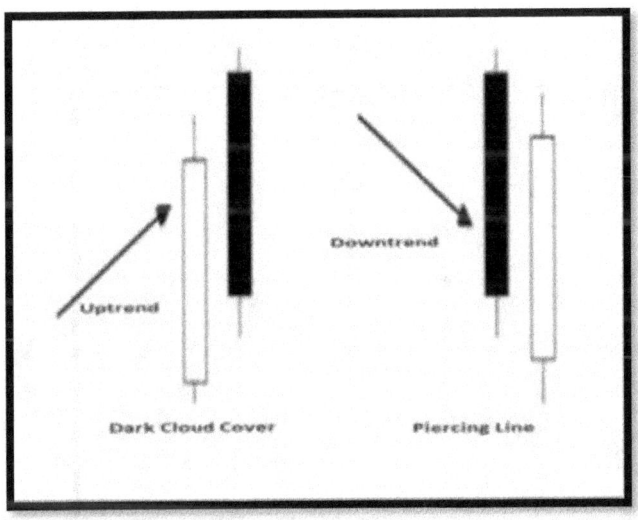

A piercing line occurs when a bullish candle closes above the middle of a bearish candle. Occurring after a downtrend, this would signal a reversal.

Doji come in a few shapes, but all will have a small body with an opening and closing price that is equal or very close to being equal. A doji will represent indecision in the market. A doji is a strong signal only when it's in a uptrend or downtrend. They could be strong signals of a change in trend.

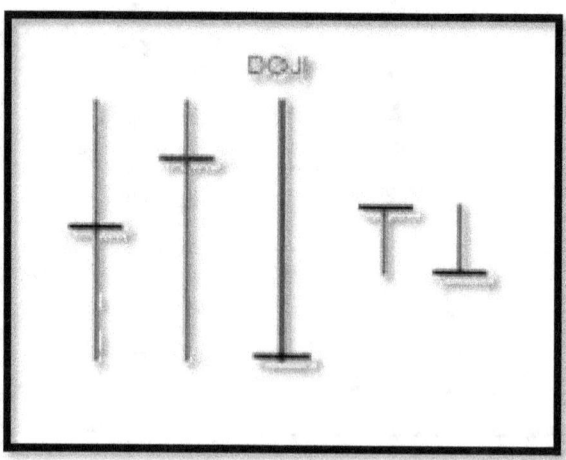

When you look at the entire collection of data points, you can get a feel for the trend. It will be an upward trend or a downward trend, typically (but could be a horizontal trend, too). This picture shows a downtrend since each previous peak is lower than the ones before it.

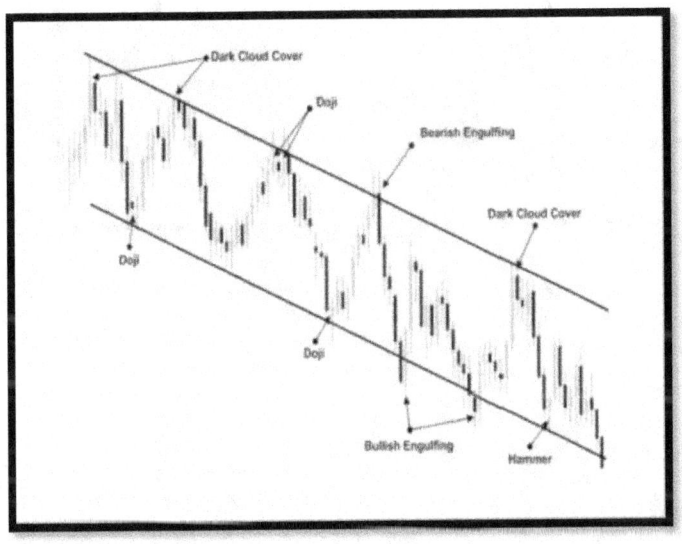

A reversal is a change in direction of the trend. The reversal can be either up or down.

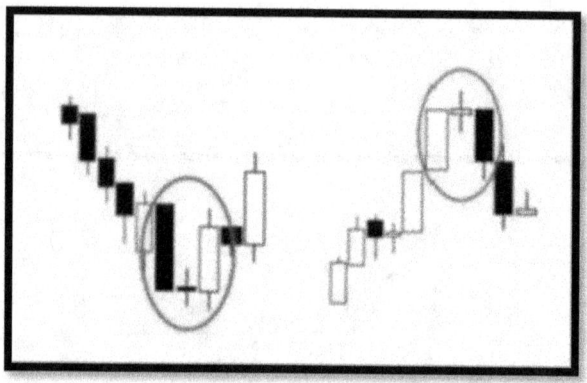

You can also have horizontal trends which occur with very little movement up or down.

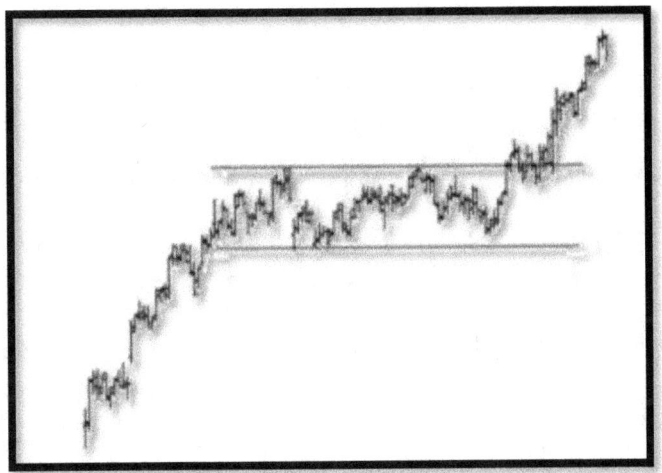

Next up would be resistance and support, which are lines that price "seldom" breaks through. Each time a price starts approaching a support or resistance, it hits an imaginary wall and will typically reverse its direction.

Support is the bottom line, and as the price starts dropping down it will approach the support line. This may be a good time to enter a long position, since you will be buying on the low swing and plan to sell as the price approaches the resistance, which is the top line that tends to bounce the price back down.

The reasons for these lines are a mix of supply and demand and psychology. Traders know what is "supposed" to happen when the price nears a support or resistance line. When the price nears the support, buyers jump in pushing the price back up. And, as it approaches the resistance sellers sell, pushing the price back down.

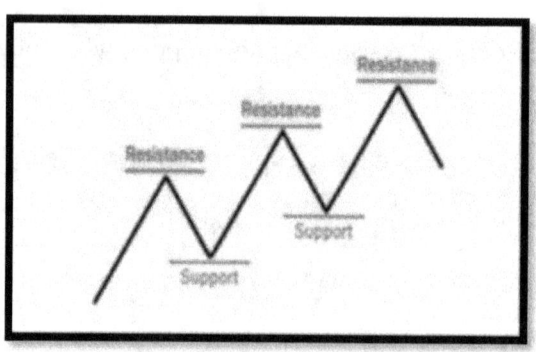

Price trends often repeat, so it's important to look at charts that go back a few days or weeks to months and years, depending on the type of trade you are making. The typical head and shoulder formation is one of the more reliable patterns to keep an eye out for in day trading.

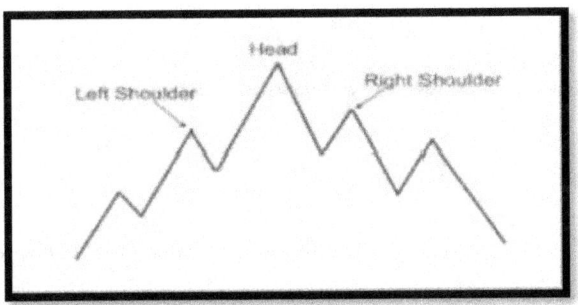

As you can see, it looks like the shoulders around a head and is a strong signal that the currency pair is about to fall once the formation is done forming, right at the shoulder line from the first shoulder.

The reverse of that is called the inverse head and shoulders which is the same formation, just upside down, and is a strong signal that the price of the currency pair is about to rise.

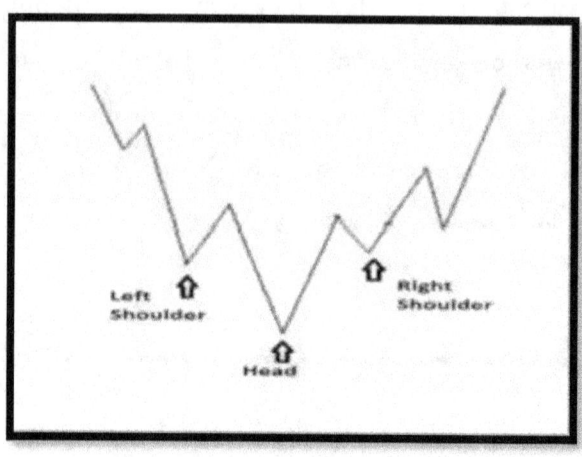

Either way a head and shoulders formation (normal or inverse) means a reversal in the trend is likely.

To go along with the body parts theme, there is also a neckline in the head and shoulders formation. The pattern is confirmed when the neckline is broken. Think of the neckline as support (standard head and shoulders) or resistance (inverse head and shoulders).

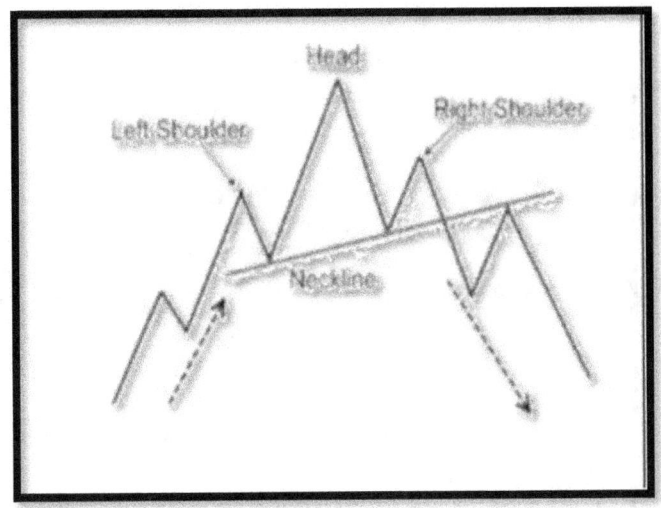

When a neckline is broken, it completes the formation of the head and shoulders, which is when most traders will take a position. The currency pair runs the risk of returning back to the previous trend, of course, and this is called a throwback. A throwback is when the price breaks the neckline then retreats back to the neckline. However, typically the neckline is a new support or resistance line and bounces the price back in the breakout direction. So if it was an inverse head and shoulders, the neckline now becomes support, helping to keep the trend in an upward direction.

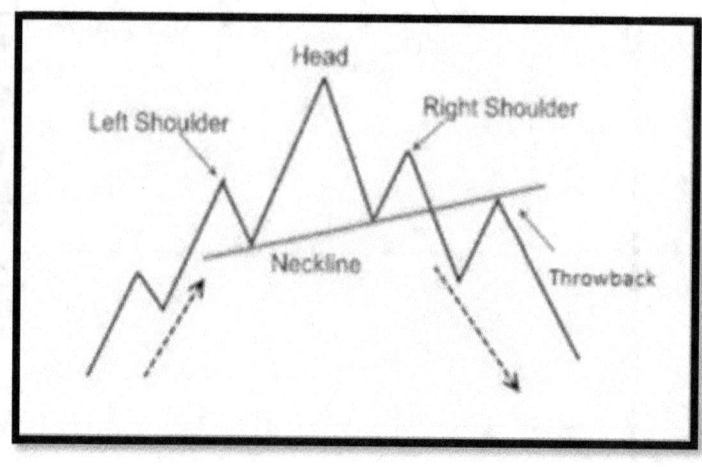

Simple moving averages (SMA) is the most popular technical indicator. It's a line that smooths out the price movement. Prices can jump all over the place and a moving average helps calm the direction of the trade down. A moving average is the average price of the currency over an amount of time. You can set it for 15, 20, 30, 50, 60,100 and 200 day periods, for example. The smaller the time period, the more sensitive. See which ones you prefer by experimenting. There is no particular one that's better than the other. In the strategy section I make recommendations, but use what fits you.

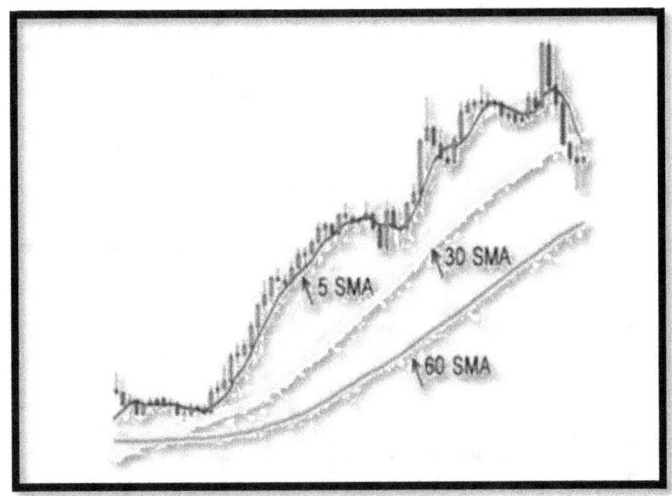

Exponential moving averages (EMA) holds more weight to the more recent prices when calculating the moving average. This is useful if there are odd spikes up or down that throw off averages. If a huge upward spike occurred a day or so ago the SMA may be thrown off, in which case you could use an EMA.

It's not uncommon to plot both or have a SMA 20 and an SMA 50 or others on the same chart.

Double top patterns are normally formed in uptrends. New highs are formed, which are followed by a small pullback. This is a frequent pattern found in hourly and daily charts. The double top is found in an uptrend where a new high is formed, followed by a small pullback. The 2nd peak doesn't need to match the first perfectly. It can be slightly higher or lower. A double top is a strong indication of a trend that is weakening and buying interest is decreasing.

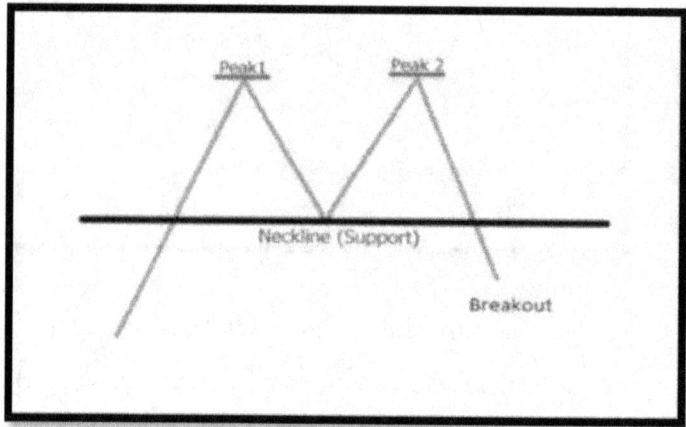

The double bottom is the opposite of the double top. This pattern forms during a downtrend and is a signal of an upcoming uptrend. Since it's upside down, it kind of looks like a "W." The confirmation of the pattern happens when the price breaks through the resistance line.

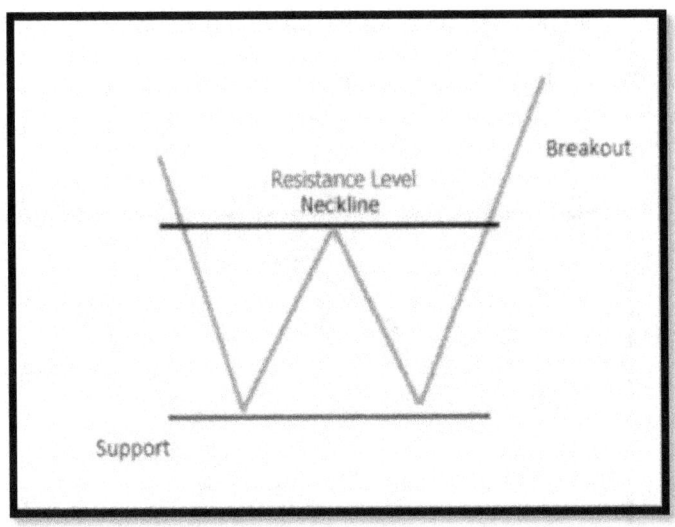

Bollinger Bands are technical indicators. They look like two lines that sandwich the market price. Bollinger Bands are great at figuring out if the currency pair is overbought or oversold. Most traders buy when the price hits the lower band and sell when the price hits the upper band.

However, the bands are not signals to buy or sell. The price is said to "walk" the bands. If you use the bands as signals alone and sell as it approaches the top band, you could be missing out as the price walks the band for awhile. As with all indicators, they must be used with other measures to gauge the market.

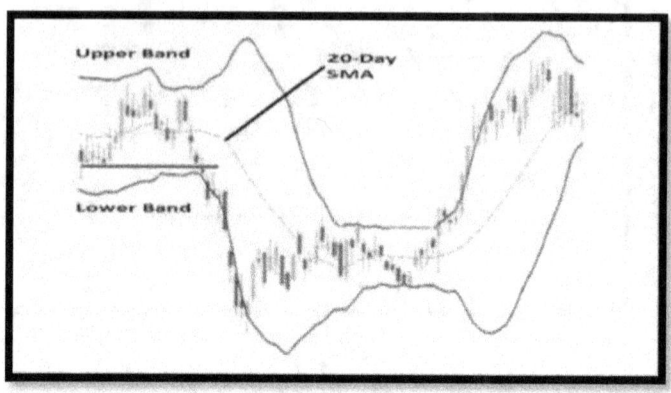

A calculation based on the difference between the currency's 26-day and 12-day EMA is called the MACD. This acts as a signal to buy or sell. When price moves above its nine-day EMA, it's a buy signal. When price moves below its nine-day EMA, it sends a sell signal.

The MACD histogram is a visual of the difference between the MACD and it's nine-day EMA. The MACD histogram is used to gauge momentum since it gives the speed of price movement.

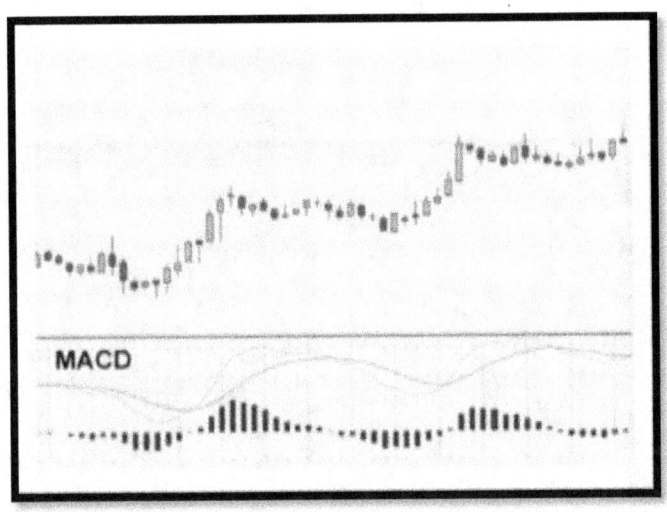

The green line is the MACD while the red line is the MACD nine-day signal line. The blue bars are the MACD Histogram.

Pennant patterns are formed when large movements start to consolidate and form converging trendlines. This is an indication that the trendline will continue in its direction at the tip of the pennant. This is great for swing traders since these formations occur from one to three weeks. If the trend was downward, it is likely it will break out of the pennant in a bearish direction again. It is the same with an upward trend continuing its bullish direction.

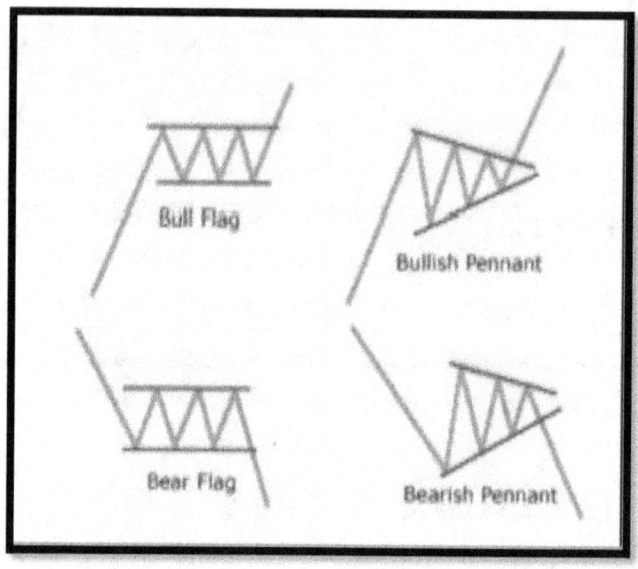

Flag patterns have two parallel lines. These lines can be flat as pictured or point in the opposite direction of the going trend. In a bullish trend the parallel lines could point toward a slight downward trend. You would usually see flag patterns after a large move, either up or down. The pattern is a "rest" before continuing in the direction of the original trend.

Diamond top formations occur at the top of a considerable uptrend. It's a strong signal of a decline. The formation can be found in any timeframe, but is especially useful for daily and hourly charts.

The pattern looks kind of like a four-sided diamond, thus the name. The rightmost side of the diamond is a strong signal of a breakout.

Ichinioku Cloud, also called the equilibrium chart, is a technical indicator that shows higher probability trades in the Forex market.

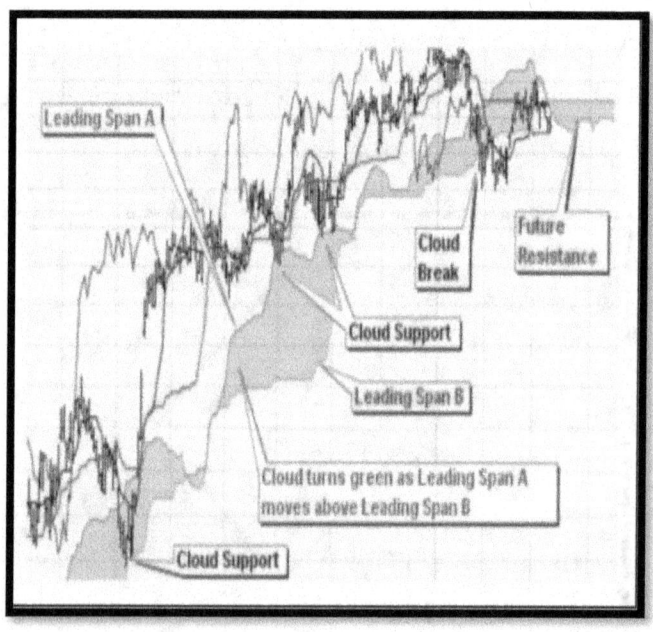

The Ichimoku chart has three lines and a cloud.

•   Conversion line is a red line that takes the highest high plus the lowest low divided by 2 and then calculated over the past seven to eight time periods.

•   Basel line is a maroon line that takes the highest high plus the lowest low divided by 2 and calculated over the past 22 time periods.

•   Lagging span is a pink line which is the most current closing price plotted 22 time periods past.

•   The cloud is made of two other lines called the Senkou Span A, which is green and the Senkou Span B, which is blue. The green line equals the red line plus the blue divided by two and plotted over 26 time periods ahead. The blue line is the same as the red and maroon lines, but it's calculated over 22 periods ahead.

The cloud known as the Kumo is used much like support and resistance. The Kumo is particularly helpful for day traders and swing traders.

A strong buy signal happens when the red line crosses above the blue from below. A strong sell signal is when the red crosses above the blue from above.

Unique Risks of Forex & Opportunities

Trading in foreign currency is risky business. Currency markets can be volatile, and it is highly speculative. You could lose the entire amount you deposited in your Forex account in a matter of minutes if the market moves against you.

You must understand the risks before you start trading. Many of the risks are similar to those you face in the stock market, but others are unique to foreign currency trading. In this chapter, we introduce you to the risks you may face when trading currency.

Leverage Risk

All currency traders use leverage to make a profit trading currency. Leverage is the use of borrowed money in an attempt to increase the potential return of a trade. Leverage is used in the currency markets because profits are made at exchange rate differences that are only fractions of a cent, so you must trade with large sums of money in order to make a notable profit.

Banks or brokers set the amount of leverage they will offer you. This is called "buying on margin." You won't find the strict government regulations regarding margin rules that you find in margin accounts available when trading stocks or options.

When a Forex dealer or broker approves your trading account, they set the rules for how much you can borrow—your margin allowance. Most Forex dealers allow you to trade on a 1 percent margin. That means with just $1,000 you can control $100,000 worth of currency. There are not many markets in which you will find that level of leverage, but remember increased leverage means you also have the potential to lose more money.

While trading hundreds of thousands of dollars may sound very exciting, remember that when you trade at these high volumes, even a minor mistake can wipe out all you have deposited in your account in a matter of minutes. Don't rush into trading your money. Read, take a course or two, and practice trading with a demonstration account before you start trading your hard-earned money. Never put more money at risk than you can afford to lose.

When you pick a pair of currencies you want to trade, the difference in the price at which you can buy and sell the currencies is just fractions of a cent. Each of these fractions is called a pip. For example, when you trade a standard lot in the currency pair EUR/USD, you can gain or lose $10 per pip. So if you buy five standard lots of 100,000 units (a total of 500,000), you could gain or lose $50 per pip.

When trading a lot size of 100,000 of any currency pair that is quoted out to 4 decimal places, the pip value will always be 10 units of the counter currency. If the counter currency is the same as the currency in which the account is funded, each pip will equal 10 units of the deposit currency. For example, for a trader with an account funded in U.S. dollars, one pip equals $10 on a 100,000 lot of EUR/USD. In cases where the counter currency is different than the currency the trader's account is funded in, each pip will still be worth 10 units, but it will have to be converted to the currency in which the account is funded to determine actual profit or loss amount.

If you are using 1 percent leverage and trade five lots, you would need to have $1,000 for each lot. Therefore, you would need $5,000 in your trading account.

Let's assume you bought five standard lots of this pair at the exchange rate of 1.2522 and it dropped by 100 pips to 1.2422 by the time you were able to sell it. Your loss would be $5,000—a complete wipeout. Even a drop of just 10 pips, from 1.2522 to 1.2512, would be a loss of $500 or 10 percent of your money. Of course, using the same scenario, you stand to gain $5,000 if the currency moves in your direction with a 100 pip swing.

Market Risk

All traders, no matter what you are trading—currency, stock, options, or futures—face market risk. Market risk basically encompasses any price movement that impacts your trade unfavorably.

From the moment you first place your trade to the moment you successfully exit it, you are facing the risk that the price of the currency may move against your position. Of course, you're hoping that the market will move in your favor, but you can never be sure that it will.

When it comes to currency, there are two key factors that impact currency values— exchange rates and interest rates—so of course these both represent a type of risk for currency traders.

Exchange Rate Risk

Whenever you open a trade involving currency, whether you are trading through the Forex spot or forward market or using options or futures transactions, you face exchange rate risk. You are immediately exposed to the possibility that the exchange rate for the currency pair you've chosen will move against your position.

Exchange rates change every few seconds, so a loss due to exchange rate risk can happen very quickly. In just a few seconds, a profitable transaction can turn into a loss.

Major global corporations manage their exchange rate risks in many different ways. Most seek to manage their exchange rate risk by buying options to hedge their bets against a change in exchange rates as they buy and sell raw materials or finished products around the world. About 5 percent of global corporations even speculate in currency trading. For example, Caterpillar turned losses in its core businesses into profits through its currency trading operations when the company was having a bad year in 1986. Its $ 100-million profit in foreign exchange trading turned its $24-million operating loss into a $76-million net profit.

Interest Rate Risk

The exchange rate is not the only the currencies you hold. A change thing that can impact the value of in interest rates by the central bank that manages the currency for the country can dramatically affect your currency positions involving the country whose rate was changed.

For example, every time the Federal Reserve decides to raise or lower interest rates, the value of the U.S. dollar will be affected.

Generally, when a central bank announces an interest rate increase, the announcement will drive up the value of a currency because the higher rates increase demand for the currency. Conversely, a decrease in interest rates likely will result in selling of that currency, so it will likely drop in value due to the lower interest rate.

Counterparty Risk

When trading currency, you'll always face counterparty risk. Whenever you enter into a currency transaction, there must be two parties involved; one party is selling and the other party is buying. The person or entity with which you are trading is called the counterparty.

Whenever you trade with another party, you risk the possibility that the other party will not be able to meet his or her obligations. This is called counterparty risk.

You can avoid this risk by trading only with known entities with excellent credit ratings. You should investigate any entity that you intend to work with as a currency trader by researching whether any problems have been reported, such as insolvency or questions of ethical conduct.

Volatility Risk

Currency prices change every second, so you can see movement in a currency thousands of times per day. This makes currency trading a very volatile endeavor. Volatility is a key part of the currency trading experience, which can be an opportunity or a risk.

If volatility in a market scares you, you probably want to think about another way to make your money. There is absolutely no way to completely avoid volatility risk when you trade foreign currencies. The good news is that you can minimize your volatility risk by sticking to the major currency pairs involving the developed countries.

Many global corporations hire currency traders to manage their foreign exchange operations. With the large amounts of money they trade each year, they can earn hefty profits for the company by speculating and taking advantage of the volatility of the markets. For example, in 1992 there were many stories about how computer company Dell was speculating in foreign currency. Dell refused to comment on it, so financial analysts scoured its financial statements to figure out whether or not this was true. No one succeeded in proving it one way or another until one of Dell's foreign exchange traders was looking for a job and the press found out he had indicated on his resume that he had traded $1 billion in currency contracts.

Liquidity Risk

You won't likely face liquidity risk when trading any of the major currency pairs. Over $1.9 trillion are traded daily, so you're not likely to find it difficult to get rid of a currency when you want to.

But (of course there's a but), if you do decide to take on more risk by trading emerging countries' currencies, liquidity risk can be a factor. Liquidity risk means that you might not be able to sell a currency you hold when you want to sell it. Of course, that is not likely to happen with the U.S. dollar, the yen, or the euro (or any other major currency), but you could have a hard time finding a buyer if you hold the currency of an emerging country. Liquidity can be particularly tricky if the country whose currency you hold just experienced a major change in political leadership—whether a violent coup or an unexpected election result.

Country Risk

When trading currency, what is happening in a particular country could greatly impact the value of its currency. There are a number of different types of country risks— political risk, regulation risk, legal risk, and holiday risk.

Some companies must operate regularly in countries that face hyperinflation or during a period of war. Managing foreign exchange trading can be crucial to their ability to operate profitably in these difficult environments. For example, in the 1980s and 1990s, Union Carbide Corporation had a task force of 30 people who managed currency operations throughout the corporation. Operating units sold their foreign currency exposures to this currency risk management unit. Dow Chemical bought Union Carbide in 2001 and the currency risk management is done through the parent company.

Political Risk

Political risk involves the stability of the country's government. As long as you stick to trading currency from countries whose governments are relatively stable, you won't face severe problems with political risk. Even if a developed country faces a major change in political leaders, it's not likely the currency will face a dramatic shift in price, but you will likely see some price movement depending upon the new leader's economic policies and the expected impact of the new leader on the country's economy.

When emerging countries face major political turmoil, you will most likely see a drop in the value of that country's currency as people try to sell it in order to get out before an even bigger fall. If you are trading the currency of an emerging country that does not have a large volume of sales even before the change in political leadership, you likely will face not only the political risk, but also liquidity risk as you try to sell.

For example, Mexico's closely fought presidential race in 2006 could have driven the value of the peso down dramatically if the leftist party leader had won the race. Instead, Mexico's currency surged after Felipe Calderon won because he pledged to continue the economic policies of Vicente Fox, which the capital markets have supported.

Operating in a war zone can be particularly difficult for a company. Halliburton has been doing just that as it supports the U.S. military in its operations overseas. In its 2002 annual report, Halliburton stated that it does not trade currency for speculation, but does for operations. It also talks about the difficulty of working with nontraded currencies. When operating in a country where currency cannot be traded, Halliburton states that it prices its products and services in these countries to attempt to cover the cost of exchange rate devaluations. Halliburton reported that it historically incurred transaction losses in its nontraded currencies.

Regulation Risk

If a government changes regulations that impact a country's currency, you face the potential of a loss because of regulation risk. Sometimes, especially when you are trading currencies involving emerging countries, the central bank will change a regulation that makes it more difficult for you to trade that currency.

For example, if you are a foreigner who holds currency in a country that changes its regulations to make it more difficult for you to hold the currency of that country, you may be forced into a position of selling the currency no matter what the loss may be to you. If you do decide to trade currencies of emerging countries, be sure you carefully research its current and potential future regulations.

You are not likely to face regulation risk in currencies of major developed nations. These currencies have been trading unimpeded on the spot market for years and are not likely to be impacted by changes in regulations.

Legal Risk

You face legal risks whenever you do business outside the country in which you live. When currency trading is involved, you often trade with a counterparty that does not reside in the same country as you do. If the counterparty were to default on the deal, you could face a legal risk depending upon which country has jurisdiction over the contract. How the contract can be enforced will depend on that jurisdiction.

If the host country of the counterparty enforces contract law differently than your home country, you could find it difficult to resolve the question. In fact, the host country could even determine that your contract was invalid or illegal. You can lose your entire position in that host country's currency.

Be sure you know who you are buying from and under which country's law the contract will be mediated if there is a problem. If you find out that U.S. contract law will not be the prevailing law, be certain you understand the law of the country that will prevail if there are any problems before you get involved in the deal.

As long as you work with a retail broker or dealer who is registered and regulated by the National Futures Association or the Commodity Futures Trading Commission, you likely will never have to worry about legal risk. But if you decide to trade with a broker or dealer not based in the United States or not regulated by the NFA or CFTC, this risk could become a big problem if you have trouble enforcing a contract.

Holiday Risk

Each country celebrates different holidays on different days. Holiday risk involves the possibility that the currency you wish to trade cannot be traded because of a bank holiday in that country. Different religious, political, or government holidays can stop the trading in the currency if the banks are closed. That could mean you can't get your money when you want it, and you will have to wait for the banks to reopen after the holiday.

When trading foreign currency, be sure you know the key holiday celebrations when the banks will be closed and plan your trading around these holidays.

Money Management Strategies

We're sure you've heard stories of people making millions of dollars trading Forex in a matter of hours or even minutes. While that may have happened for a lucky few, more often than not you won't be seeing that kind of win. You could even lose more than the total balance in your Forex account in a matter of minutes if you're not careful.

In this chapter, we talk about how to manage your money and how to develop a disciplined trading plan. We also discuss the importance of keeping your emotions in check, as well as risk-management strategies.

Developing a Money-Management Plan

When you decide to trade Forex, you're trading with the big boys—central banks, international financial institutions, and major corporations. You also need to think big and understand where trading Forex fits with your portfolio-management strategies. First, ask yourself these three questions:

• Do I understand the foreign exchange market fully, as well as the risks I'll be taking?

• Does trading Forex fit with my long-term portfolio-management strategies?

• Can I spend the time needed to research this market daily and make sound Forex trading decisions?

If your answer is "no" to any of these questions, you're not ready to trade Forex.

That said, if you can answer "yes," then think of Forex money management as you would if you were managing any other business.

Develop a business plan. Determine how much money you want to risk, what return you expect to make, and how much time you will be able to devote to the business. We recommend that you start trading with no more than about 2 percent of your portfolio assets. When you are confident that you know what you are doing, you can increase that to 5 percent. You probably would not want to put more than 5 percent of your portfolio assets in such a risky business venture. As you decide on your return expectations, remember that even the best money managers aim for a goal of 15 to 20 percent annual return over the long term.

Set up your business office. You should determine what physical assets your business will have, including your workspace and computer equipment. The more structured you make your business surroundings, the greater control you will have over your business activities. Don't set up your business periodically on your dining room table. If that's all you can afford to do, you're not ready for serious trading. You will need a quiet space where you can research your trades and develop your charts.

View your holdings as inventory. The currency pairs you hold should be treated like inventory, something you plan to buy and sell. Don't get emotionally tied to your inventory.

Accept your mistakes. Every business person makes mistakes as they are building a business. That's true for Forex traders as well. Don't try to defend a trading mistake. Take your loss and move on. If your choice no longer makes good business sense, make that cold, hard decision to exit the position before a small loss turns into a big one— which can happen in seconds when market conditions are volatile.

Take your profits. When you have a healthy profit and reach your exit point, don't hold on to the inventory. No one can accurately pick the top or bottom of any trade every time. Don't push your luck; follow your business plan.

Stick to your trading plan. Once you pick a trading strategy, stick with your plan. Don't change it in the middle of the trade if things go sour. Follow your plan and then assess your mistake so you won't make it again. Many traders learn more from their mistakes than their successes.

Taking Steps to Discipline Your Trades

Every Forex trader needs to develop a sound trading strategy that they can follow regularly. We won't recommend a specific strategy. That's something you need to develop for yourself based on your own emotional tendencies, as well as your knowledge and understanding of the marketplace.

Here are the 5 steps to developing your trading plan:

Step 1: Take a macroeconomic view. Start your research by looking at the economic conditions around the world. What are the key pressures driving economic forces— including wars, oil prices, trade agreements among nations, storms, earthquakes, or holiday shopping? Look at whether the economy is being viewed globally in a generally pessimistic (most people expect things to get worse) or optimistic (most people expect things to get better) way. One of the easiest ways to judge this quickly is to watch one of the business cable news networks.

Step 2: Find news about specific money market conditions. Start focusing on what is happening in the money markets. If something could dramatically affect the money markets, all the business analysts will be talking about it. For example, if there is going to be a major rate meeting by one of the key central banks, such as the Federal Reserve in the United States or the Bank of England, we can guarantee there will be much speculation about what the central bank might do regarding a possible rate increase or decrease.

Once you've completed Steps 1 and 2, you should have a good idea of what the market sentiment is around the world, as well as in the countries on which you plan to focus your attention.

Step 3: Pick your currency pairs. Once you have a good understanding of the currency market, you will be able to pick the currency pairs you wish to trade. You want to focus on pairs that may be volatile that day, week, or month—whatever your trading horizon might be. Decide which economic indicators will be the most important for market moves during the window of your trading plan. Also look at the recent trends in prices for the currency pairs you're considering trading. Do you see a strong trend or do you see a lot of volatility (no clear direction)? Use this step to narrow down the potential currency pairs for which you expect to set up a trading plan.

Step 4: Determine your basic technical points. Start using your favorite chart types to look for signs of support (a point on your chart at which sellers won't let the price fall below as they start buying the currency pair) and resistance (a point on the chart at which buyers won't let the price go above as they stop buying the currency pair). Use this information to pick currency pairs you want to trade based on the direction in which you expect the market to move. The fundamental information you gathered in Step 2 will help confirm the trends you are seeing in your charts.

Step 5: Pick your entry and exit points. Fine-tune your trading plan by actually picking your entry and exit points. If you look at the charts and still don't know how to do that, you need to spend more time learning how to apply technical analysis. As you become more comfortable with it, you'll pick the tools that best match your trading style and your knowledge or abilities. You must know both your entry and exit points before you even try to make the trade. Determine your plan and stick to it!

As you are learning how to use the inverted pyramid method, test your successes or failures with the method by opening a demonstration account with a Forex broker.

Getting Your Emotions in Check

When trading, your emotions can jump up and down almost as quickly as the market. While you can't deny your emotions, the key is to keep them under control so you can stick to your plan. But some people don't have the emotional stamina to even try to trade.

Ask yourself these questions:

• Does the idea of losing money keep you up at night?

• Can you not read the financial news without reacting emotionally?

• Do you make trading decisions quickly based on the latest tip you've heard?

If you answered "yes" to these questions, you probably don't have the emotional make-up to be a successful Forex trader. Forex traders must remain calm and focused on their plans. They must research the currency pairs they watch regularly. It is best if you can set aside time to watch the market daily, even if you don't plan to trade daily. By paying close attention to moves in the markets on a daily, consistent basis, you will be able to understand when there is a long-term trend driving the market or when the market takes a different direction.

One of the hardest things for some traders to do is to sell a position they are attached to. Don't get too attached. Remember that it is a business. You write a business plan (trading plan) and you follow that plan. Don't let your emotions take control and get you to alter your plans.

We know that can be easier said than done. You spend days, weeks, or months researching the markets and finally develop a strategy and plan that works for you.

If your plan works brilliantly, you have a sizeable profit. Now it's time to sell or buy according to your plan. But you just can't break away. You may want to ride the trade to the top, but don't. The fall can be quick and you could lose all you gained. Don't let your emotions drive your trading decisions; let your plan be your guide.

Emotions can also make it hard for you to sell, even if the exit point you set to minimize a loss is approaching quickly. You just can't figure out how you were so wrong and don't want to admit to a mistake. You still think it's a good trade and you want to hold on just a bit longer to try to prove yourself right. Don't do it. Letting go can be hard to do, but keep yourself focused on your plan and don't let your emotions take control.

Most Forex brokers offer commission-free trades. It's not like trading stock, where you must worry about the costs of getting in and out of a position. Get out, take your profits, or accept your losses. It doesn't cost you anything to re-enter the trade if you decide that's what you want to do.

Then take a deep breath. Take another look at your plan and determine whether you still think it's a good one and if you might consider different points for entering and exiting a new trade that reflects the recent market moves.

Do a calm, focused job of researching your position again. If a position moved much differently than you expected, do more research to see what might be different in both fundamental and technical analysis assumptions. It could be that a major economic shock that you missed took control of the markets after you set your plan.

Try to find the reason for the difference from your expectations. Even if you aren't going to trade that pair again in the next day, week, or month, understand why you made a mistake so you don't repeat your mistake again in the future.

Risk-Management Strategies

The best way to manage your risk is by setting up orders to take your profits when you first open your position. That way you don't risk getting caught up emotionally in the winning moment and ride your profits to a loss.

Set up stop-loss orders when you first open your position. That way your logic will be in control rather than your greed or emotional disappointment if the trade doesn't go as planned.

The Language of International Currency

As a Forex trader, you'll be placing orders either to buy or sell currency. The basic process is not difficult, but you do need to understand certain terms unique to trading.

In this chapter, we review the trading terms for placing an order, explain the process of borrowing money to buy money, sort out how to pick your broker or dealer, review the basics of placing an order, and explore the types of orders.

Reviewing Key Trading Terms

If you've traded stocks, you'll find many of the terms for trading Forex to be similar, but with a slightly different twist. This section covers some key terms you should be sure you understand before placing an order.

Long/Short

When you first enter the Forex market you either go long by buying a currency or go short by selling a currency. When a currency is going up, you want to buy that currency so you go long. For example, if after researching currencies you learn that euros are expected to increase in value relative to the U.S. dollar, you would buy euros and sell U.S. dollars.

The opposite is true if your research shows that a currency is expected to decrease in relative value. Then you would short the currency by selling it and buying one that is expected to rise.

Positions

A position is an open trade. Every time you take a position in the Forex market, it involves someone buying and selling each currency in the pair while someone else has to be willing to sell and buy the corresponding currencies.

You should have no trouble trading a currency pair as long as there is liquidity in the market for that pair. If you are trading the major currencies, you should be able to find a willing buyer or seller, called a counterparty.

You will usually close out a position with your broker by reversing the original transaction. For example, if you bought Japanese yen with U.S. dollars, you would close the trade by selling Japanese yen for U.S. dollars.

Bid/Offer

When you see a quote for a currency pair, you will actually see two prices. One is the price at which the Forex broker or dealer is willing to sell the currency, which is called the offer or the ask. The other is the price at which the Forex market maker is willing to buy the currency, which is called the bid. This can also be viewed in terms of the trader, where the bid is the price at which a customer can sell, and the offer is the price at which a customer can buy. The bid price is always lower than the offer price, and is listed as the first price in a quote.

Spread

The spread is the difference in pips between the bid and the ask price for a currency. Forex brokers and dealers make money from the spread rather than with commissions, so you may notice a difference in the size of the spreads offered by different brokers, dealers, and banks.

Most brokers and dealers advertise that you can trade Forex commission-free because they make their money on the spread. Be sure you understand how the broker or dealer is being compensated before opening an account. Most spreads result in a cost of $10 to $40 per trade. Some Forex brokers hide additional fees in a wide spread, so review the spread carefully with your broker and be sure you understand your trading costs. Always look for a broker or dealer who consistently offers tight spreads (which means the bid and ask are close in price)— especially on the major currency pairs. It will save you money.

Exchange Rate

Exchange rates are given in terms of the base currency and pricing (or terms) currency. The base currency is always shown first in a currency pair. If you are buying the base currency, the exchange rate is the amount you would pay or receive depending on the value of the base currency in terms of the pricing currency. Conversely, if you are selling the base currency, the exchange rate is how much you'll pay or receive for one unit of that currency.

For example, if the pair is shown as USD/JPY, the U.S. dollar is the base currency and the Japanese yen is the terms currency. So a quote of USD/JPY to sell USD for JPY at a price of 114.72 would mean for each US dollar you could get 114.72 Japanese yen.

In Forex trading, the exchange rate will always be given as a pair when you are buying or selling because you are always selling one currency to buy another.

Pip

A pip is the pricing unit used in Forex trading. A pip is the smallest change in price that can be made in a currency. It is one unit of price change in the bid/ask price of a currency and is denoted by the last number behind the decimal point of the price. For example, if you receive a quote for the pair USD/JPY (U.S. dollar/Japanese yen) of 114.78/114.81, the spread is 3 pips.

Bull/Bear

When a market is described as a bull market, the general market is moving upward. If the bears are in control of a market, then the general market is moving downward.

Leverage

If you want to make money trading Forex, you'll most likely need to borrow money because the price differences in currency, which are what you will make your profit or loss on, are only fractions of a cent. When you borrow money to trade, it is called leverage.

Leverage is the amount of money a Forex broker or dealer will lend you for your trading activities. A common leverage option is 100 to 1. That means for every unit you use of your own capital, the broker will lend you 100 units. So for an account with $5,000, you can trade up to $500,000 of currency.

Margin accounts can make you responsible for losses that exceed the dollar amount you put into the account. Don't trade on margin unless you understand how much money you are putting at risk. Be prepared to accept losses that can exceed the amount of money you put into a margin account. While some brokers or dealers have policies in place to take you out of the market before you reach a negative balance, it cannot always be avoided during market gaps.

While it might sound exciting that you can trade half a million dollars for just $5,000, remember that while leverage does help you maximize your profits, it also increases your risk for substantial losses. When you're first getting started in Forex, it's a good idea to start much smaller.

To avoid taking on too much risk and to be sure you'll have enough money to cover any losses, it's a good idea to limit each trade to just 5 or 10 percent of your useable margin. That way if you do take a sizeable loss, you'll have enough in your account to cover that loss without having to dig deeper into your pockets.

Watch your useable margin as you trade. As you build your account, you'll be able to buy more lots, but if you take it slowly and follow the basic rule of not putting more than 5 to 10 percent of your useable margin in one basket, you'll minimize your risk. This will allow you to diversify your currency pairs and keep better control on your loss potential. You may also have a better chance of building your account with steady profits.

If your useable funds go into the negative, you will get a margin call. This means that if you don't come up with the money required to maintain your account quickly, the positions you hold will be sold to cover your losses.

Most Forex dealers will give their clients between two and five days to cover a margin call. If you cannot bring your account up to the specified minimum, your broker or dealer has the right to sell your positions to cover your account balance. A margin call is not a bad thing—its purpose is to protect you and your capital. Be sure you read the fine print on your margin account contract. Also, discuss with your dealer how margin calls are handled and how much time you'll have to answer a call.

Be patient as you build your Forex account and don't put too much of your money into one currency pair. Follow the rule of trading no more than 5 to 10 percent of your useable margin on one transaction. You can minimize your risk and work toward steadily building your profits.

When your useable margin drops too low (that level will be set by your broker when you open an account), you won't be able to trade on your current positions. You'll get a message on your screen such as "account in untradeable condition." You'll probably need to put more money into your account in order to trade.

You can lose your entire account balance if you're not careful, but you aren't likely to lose your house on a margin call. By putting on the brakes when your useable margin falls below a certain point, a good broker is actually protecting you from a more significant loss. Although you may initially get angry when you can't trade, it's a good thing and for your own protection.

Many Forex dealers no longer use a margin call system because the market moves too fast for traders to respond. All money could be lost too quickly. Instead, dealers set a minimum margin percent requirement, such as 25 percent of the account equity. If the account falls below that percentage, all holdings are liquidated. This protects the trader from losing everything. That way the trader will have enough money left after liquidation to begin trading again.

Choosing a Broker or Dealer

When you start looking for a company to open an account with, you'll find there are hundreds of websites promising quick riches. Most will promise you commission-free trades, but watch out for the hidden costs and those that are not so hidden.

Remember that the way most brokers or dealers make

money is based on the spread between the bid and ask price. Always look for tight spreads to save money.

But more importantly, you need to find an established and reputable dealer. Forex dealers have relationships with large banks or financial institutions because of the large sums of capital that are involved.

If you do decide to work with a broker, be sure you find one that is affiliated with an FCM. An FCM can handle futures contract orders and can extend credit to customers. If based in the United States, your broker should also be registered with the Commodity Futures Trading Commission (CFTC) and can be a member of the National Futures Association (NFA).

Exploring Order Types

You can use several different types of orders to trade Forex. We're going to introduce you to the five key types—market orders, limit orders, stop orders, stop-limit orders, and order cancels order.

Market Order

A market order is the simplest and most basic order you can place. You see a trade you want and place an order to make the trade.

The problem with a market order is that you are not always guaranteed that the actual trade your broker completes will match the precise entry point that you saw on your screen. If you are trying to guarantee a particular price on execution, a market order is not a good selection.

The Forex market moves so fast that by the time your trade is executed, even if it is less than a second later, the price of the currency pair could change. The quotes you see on your screen may not be accurate because the market may have moved so fast that the price you saw no longer exists.

Limit Order

A better type of order to place when buying or selling a currency is called a limit order. This type of order allows you to specify the price at which you want to buy or sell the currency pair.

If you are looking to buy a currency, you would place a limit order specifying that you will buy the currency at a specific price or lower. That way you won't end up paying more for the currency than what you specified as the appropriate entry point.

If you are looking to sell a currency, you would place a limit order specifying that you will sell the currency at a specific price or higher. That way you won't end up with less than the price that you chose as the appropriate exit point.

Some brokers may charge more for a limit order than a market order, but this is not a place where you should be thrifty. In this type of fast-moving market, you want the extra protection of a limit order. If your broker charges too much for limit orders, find another broker, but don't cut corners by placing market orders. Most dealers, including GFT, offer limit orders at no additional charge.

There are two types of limit orders you can place— good til canceled and good for the day.

Good til Canceled (GTC) orders remain in play until you decide to cancel the order. You have the responsibility to monitor your outstanding orders, so pay close attention to your standing limit orders to be sure you do still want them to be executed.

Good for the Day (GFD) orders remain in play through the day and are automatically removed by your broker at the end of the day. Because the Forex market has the advantage of being a 24-hour market, a variation of GFD in Forex is "Good until close of." With this added twist you indicate which currency pair you want to indicate as GFD and what geographical market you want it to correspond to. For example, you might want your EUR/USD order to be canceled when the London market closes.

Stop Order

When you place a stop order, you set in place an order that will automatically be executed when your price is hit. When the price is hit, the order becomes a market order and will be executed as soon as possible.

Stop orders are used by traders to lock in profits or limit losses. For example, suppose you decided that you wanted to trade the currency pair USD/JPY. After researching your numbers, you saw that the best entry point was 116. You placed a limit order and purchased the yen for 116.

You expect the yen to gain in relative value and you want to liquidate your position when it hits 112. You see that the yen moves to a price of 114. You've picked the right direction for the currency and want to lock in your profits. You would then place a stop order at 114.5, just in case the yen starts moving in the other direction, to protect your profit. If the yen does end up losing value and heads back up to 116, your broker would automatically execute the stop order and protect your profits between 116 and 114.5.

If the currency is very volatile and moving up and down between 116 and 112, your stop order could be executed too soon. The market might make it down to your target exit point of 112, but after your stop is already executed.

Also, your stop order is not a guaranteed exit price. When the stop price is hit, it becomes a market order and will be executed at the best possible price as quickly as possible. So if the market is moving rapidly, you could end up with an order executed at a price significantly different than the price you specified in your stop order.

Stop-Limit Order

Your best bet if you want to guarantee a price is to place an order that uses the benefits of both a stop order and a limit order, called a stop-limit order. If you place a stop order, but are worried that the market may move too quickly for the order to be executed in time, then you can include a limit order as part of the stop order.

When you use a stop-limit order, the stop becomes a limit order rather than a market order and won't be executed unless your broker can get the price you specified or better.

Remember, a limit order does prevent the trade from being executed. If the market is moving so fast that your broker or dealer doesn't have enough time to execute the order at the price you specified, you could end up missing the opportunity for your order to be executed completely.

Order Cancels Order

Sometimes you'll want to use a more complicated order that actually allows you to place two limit or two stop orders at the same time. You can actually place one order to buy a currency at a specific price and one order to sell the same currency at a specific price.

For example, suppose you see the pair USD/JPY at a price of 116. In researching the currency, you saw some data indicating that there may be a breakout increasing the value of the yen to 117 and other data indicating that the yen may drop in value to 115. In this case, you might place a buy limit order at 115.5 and a sell limit order at 116.5. If the market moves toward 117, the sell limit order would be executed and the buy limit ordered would be canceled.

Trailing Stop Order

With a trailing stop order, you can set your stop order to continue to follow the price movement (in real time) by specifying the distance, in pips, you would like your stop to move—depending on the market direction and type of stop order placed.

For example, you have an open position where you bought (went long) one lot (100,000 units) of USD/JPY at 108.50. You are expecting the pair to move 50 pips to 109 but want to limit your loss should volatile market conditions move against you. You could set up an automatic trailing stop to exit your position at 108.70 (thus automatically stopping a loss).

Calculating Profits and Losses

Next, we show you how to calculate your profits or losses. After closing out a position, you take the price you paid to sell the base currency and subtract the price you paid to buy back the base currency, then multiply the difference by the transaction size. That will give you the gain or loss in the currency traded. You would then have to multiply that amount by the conversion rate of that currency to dollars to find out your gain or loss in U.S. dollars.

For example, suppose you bought USD/JPY at 114.66 and sold at 114.57. Also suppose the conversion rate from 1 yen to dollars is .0087. Here is how you would calculate your gain in yen and then convert it to dollars.

- Step 1: Subtract 114.57-114.66 = .09 pips.

- Step 2: Multiply .09 x 100,000 = Gain of 9,000 yen

- Step 3: Multiply 9,000 x .0087 − Gain of $78.30

When you have a profit, you subtract any broker's fees to calculate your profit.

If the numbers were reversed and you had bought yen for 114.57 and sold it for 114.66, then you would have had a loss of 9,000 yen or $78.30.

Mini-Accounts - The Application of Small Steps to Success

When just getting started with Forex, many people prefer to start slowly by taking tiny steps. You can do that through a mini account.

But be careful. Many mini accounts allow much higher leverage. You can lose your entire deposit in a matter of hours.

In this chapter, we explain how mini accounts work and the dangers of leveraging too much.

Starting Small

A standard lot in Forex is 100,000 units of a specific currency. So if you buy one standard lot of currency with a price of $1.2155, you would control $121,550 of that currency.

$1.2155 x 100,000 = $121,550

Most Forex dealers allow you to buy this lot on a margin account with leverage of 100:1, which translates into a 1 percent margin deposit. So you would need $1,215.50 in your Forex trading account to make this trade.

$121,550 x.01 =$1,215.50

Although this is less than the minimum deposit for standard accounts (minimum deposits typically range from $2,000 to $10,000), if you're new to Forex, that may still be more than you are ready to risk on your first purchase. To make it easier for you as a new trader, and less risky, many brokers and dealers offer what is called a mini account.

With a mini account you can buy a mini lot, which is just 10,000 units. So for the same currency exchange example discussed here you would need only a $121.55 security deposit in your account:

$1.2155 x 10,000 = $12,155

$12,155 x.01 = $121.55

You can't make much money trading that small. For example, if the price of the currency moved 100 pips to $1.2255, then it would be worth $12,255. Your profit would be $100. Essentially, with this size lot 1 pip equals $1.

Now, suppose the market moved 100 pips against you to $1.2055, then you would have just $15,055, which would be a loss of $100.

This type of movement in the Forex market can happen over a matter of hours and the amount you deposited can quickly be lost, but at least the loss on a mini account is much less than it would be for a standard lot.

In looking at the same scenario with a standard lot, you would initially control $121,550 with a deposit of $1,215.50. If the market moved in your favor by 100 pips, the lot would be worth:

$1.2255 \times 100,000 = \$122,550$

Your profit would be $1,000 less any broker fess.

But, just as quickly, the market could move against by 100 pips to 1.2055, and then your lot would be worth:

$1.2055 \times 100,000 = \$120,550$

Your loss would be $1,000 plus any broker fees.

You may not be ready to take that much risk if you're just starting out with Forex trading. You're better off using a mini account initially and making your mistakes by taking less risk. While you won't gain much, use the time trading in a mini account to learn the ropes and test your trading strategies.

By using smaller lot sizes, you'll build up your account slowly. But if you do things right you can build your trading account to a sizeable amount before building the confidence to try your strategies trading standard account sizes.

Mini accounts allow you to start small, but don't use that advantage to leverage your purchases too much. While some brokers or dealers allow you to leverage 400:1, don't

do it unless you're confident that you know what you are doing. With leverage that high, you can quickly lose more than you spent to initially enter the trade.

Risks of Over-Leveraging

You'll find many brokers out there offer not only mini accounts, but mini accounts with starting deposits of as little as $250 or $300. You may wonder how you could start trading with so little and still be able to avoid putting all your eggs in one basket.

So how can you really learn anything starting with such a small deposit? Brokers or dealers that allow you to start with such a small account also permit you to leverage your money 400:1, which can be very risky. The minimum deposit in this case is calculated by 0.25 percent or by multiplying your lot value by 0.0025.

Using the same numbers again, here's what you would need to have on deposit for a 10,000 unit mini lot when buying a currency worth $1.2155 with 400:1 margin.

10,000 x $1.2155 x .0025 = $30.39

Now that looks better if you only deposited $250. You might think you could actually carry out about five or six trades at that level.

But don't get too excited. First think about what happens to your money with that type of leverage if you experience a 100 pip loss. When you leverage 400:1, you still experience the same loss, but you're putting up less money.

You're still in control of the same amount of currency: 10,000 x $1.2155 = $12,155

If the currency drops 100 pips, it will be worth $1.2055, so you will now be holding currency worth:

10,000 x $1.2055 = $12,055

So the amount that you spent to buy the currency on margin with just $30.39 has now lost $100 plus. So you've lost more money than you put into the trade.

If you only have $250 on deposit and you experience two losses like this, which can happen very quickly when you are new to trading Forex, your account can be wiped out much more quickly with a 400:1 margin.

Don't Start Too Small!

If you see a margin rate of 400:1, make sure you have a good idea of what you are doing. If you're not ready to put at least $2,500 into starting your Forex trading business, start practicing with a demonstration account and wait until you are ready to make at least that level of commitment.

But don't ever go deeper into your pockets and then use money that you intended for your child's education or your retirement in such a risky venture. You must always be ready to lose all the money in a Forex account, especially when you are first beginning and learning all the tools you'll need— fundamental analysis, technical analysis, and charting.

Take the time to learn and save your risk capital. It will be time well spent to get yourself ready for this opportunity to make a lot of money trading money. But be ready to lose a lot at times, too.

Even the most experienced traders can take a loss when the market moves against their expectations. You can never be immune to periodic losses if you choose to trade Forex.

Some brokers who offer mini accounts will even allow inexperienced traders to open an account using a credit card. This can be extremely risky. Not only can you lose all the money you deposit using a cash advance from your credit card, you would then also be paying high interest rates as you pay back your credit card company, increasing your potential for loss.

Always trade Forex using cash you have deposited. If you use your credit card, you could lose the money you deposited even before you get your credit card bill.

Carefully Check Out Your Loss Potential

When you sign up with a broker, check the small print on your account agreement. Be sure the agreement limits your losses to the amount that you deposit. That means that you should never lose more than you put into your account, except in times of extreme market gapping, when the market is very volatile, such as after a major earthquake.

Before depositing any money, read all the fine print carefully. You must understand your rights and responsibilities, as well as the obligations of your broker.

Some brokers promoting mini accounts do so to lure unsuspecting clients into taking more risk than they can truly afford to take. These brokers often don't have the training or the financial ability to even understand how speculative the Forex market truly can be. Don't be one of their victims. Educate yourself fully before beginning to trade.

If you're drawn into the market by high-pressure sales without taking the time to truly learn how to trade Forex successfully, you're doomed to fail and lose all the money you deposit. You could even possibly lose more than you deposit.

Many Forex brokers that offer these low minimum accounts limit their risks but increase yours. Their computer trading software includes built-in liquidation stop losses.

If your trade moves against you, the broker's software is written to automatically limit its risk. When your account falls below a certain level, the broker's computer software is programmed to automatically sell your positions to cover your margin call.

When you get a margin call, your holdings can be closed immediately if your account agreement is set up with that type of provision. You could lose your entire account in minutes. Your broker won't lose, though. He's protected himself by putting in these automatic stop losses.

Your losses are locked in because your positions were closed. Your broker is fully protected with the automatic stop losses.

Very high leverage can help you build your small account in a hurry. But it's a double-edged sword. You can also end up burning through your deposit just as quickly if the market moves against you. Concentrate on the size of the risk you are taking on each trade rather than the amount of currency you're going to control.

Test out a number of scenarios based on the way the market may move, just as we did previously. Run the numbers for a 100, 200, or 300 pip gain or loss. Be sure you can handle that level of loss and still be able to trade again. If not, you're probably leveraging too high. Take it slower.

Learn, make your mistakes without taking on too much risk, and give yourself the time to become an experienced, successful Forex trader. You will always find currency to trade. It's much harder to rebuild an account that you've lost completely to trading mistakes.

Who The Players Are, Their Systems, and How To Get Them To Work For You

You might be interested in trying Forex trading, but you don't have the time to research and manage a Forex account by yourself. You do have several options—working with a professional manager, opening an account with a hedge fund that specializes in trading Forex, or using a managed trading system. In this chapter, we review the pros and cons of the managed Forex options.

Professional Forex Managers

Professional Forex managers used to be available only to individuals who had at least $100,000 in their Forex account. Today, some dealers can make arrangements for you to open an account with a professional Forex manager with an initial deposit of as little as $10,000.

Trading Forex requires you to research not only the actual currencies you want to trade, but also all the countries involved in those trades. It can be an enormous task and requires a full-time commitment if you want to do it well.

Picking a well-respected professional Forex manager can help you to develop a well-diversified Forex portfolio using disciplined and proven trading skills. Your manager will have experience seeing profits in both rising and falling markets.

The key of course is to find the right manager. Don't try to do that by researching options completely on your own using the Internet. You'll find hundreds of websites promising professional Forex management, but many are scams.

Seek out advice from trusted friends and associates who have worked with a professional Forex manager and can recommend him highly. Also get recommendations from Forex brokers with whom you are considering opening an account.

Don't ever choose a professional Forex manager solely by doing an Internet search, finding an interesting website, and opening a new account online. Be sure to do extensive research on the broker or dealer who has the site as well as the professional Forex manager recommended.

Seek out a professional manager who has years of consistent of Forex trading experience, as well as a solid group of traders working for him. Many top professional Forex managers have developed proprietary technical trading strategies that analyze and predict various trends in the foreign exchange markets.

As you research potential Forex managers, be sure you understand their strategies and whether they might work well for you. For example, a professional manager's experience and research may enable him to spot recurring price patterns that he has learned to take advantage of to make profits.

Most professional Forex managers have complex computer programs that help them manage the funds. These programs automatically monitor holdings for predetermined risk-management factors. These factors will provide a signal for entering and exiting positions at the appropriate time based on the parameters set by the manager.

Research how long the manager usually holds on to his trades. You will find some managers who are day traders closing out all positions at the end of the trading day, some who hold trades one to five days, and some who keep positions open up to 20 days or longer.

Of course, you will have to pay a fee to the manager. A common fee structure is 25 percent of trading profits plus a 2 percent annual management fee. Be prepared to give up a significant portion of your gains, because convenience comes at a cost. Be sure you understand the fees you will pay before opening an account with a professional manager.

Hedge Funds

You can also get into the Forex market by seeking out hedge funds that specialize in trading Forex. Hedge funds are not regulated in the same way as mutual funds, so when choosing a hedge fund, research it carefully. The government regulations for hedge funds are minimal and do little to protect the investor up front.

You will most likely need at least $100,000 to buy into a managed hedge fund account. In other words, hedge funds are only for people who can afford to risk a sizeable amount of their cash.

You will hear stories of people investing hundreds of thousands of dollars, or even millions, in a hedge fund that goes broke and they lose everything. These are highly risky investment vehicles.

Hedge funds, like professional Forex managers, expect significant rewards for their services. Expect fund fees of 25 percent of net profits, which means that you subtract unrealized losses from unrealized gains to find the net profit. They also usually get a 2 percent annual fee for managing the hedge fund portfolio.

The primary benefit of a hedge fund is its diversification, which means the variety of currency pairs and other investments they may hold at any given time. You will find a statement of methodology when you begin researching the hedge fund. That's where you'll discover the fund manager's trading style.

When you get information from the hedge fund, look for details about how many different currency pairs are traded by the fund and in what geographic areas the fund concentrates its research. Be sure the regional areas of interest match your trading goals. For example, if you want to focus on currency trades in the European market, you don't want to open an account with a hedge fund that focuses on the Asian market with only a small portion of its portfolio in the European markets. In addition, you should find out how long the fund usually holds on to its trades. A fund that closes out its trades daily will likely be more volatile than one that tends to hold winning trades longer.

You should also see a statement about how the manager controls risk and what strategies he uses to minimize risk. While all Forex trading is risky, there are strategies one can take to minimize that risk. You also should look for some discussion about the volatility of the fund. Can you live with those ups and downs? Or will the fund's volatility make you so nervous that you ask to get out at one of the worst times of performance?

Managed Accounts and Trading Systems

Another way to get into the Forex market if you're not ready or able to make the full-time commitment to trade is by using trading systems or managed accounts. Automated trading systems will give you a signal when it's a good time to enter or exit a trade.

Managed Accounts

Managed accounts can be an alternative to hiring a

professional manager or buying into

a hedge fund. For these types of accounts, you open an account in your name and then take advantage of an automated trading system developed by the account manager.

Managed Forex accounts are not registered as separate investment products with the U.S. Securities and Exchange Commission. As long as Forex is the only asset traded, an account manager doesn't have to officially provide disclosure documents.

Documents you can expect to find with other types of SEC-registered products include information about strategy, audited performance, and fees. Even if the information isn't required, be sure to get it anyway. If you can't get the answers you want, run—don't walk—away.

Some brokers who offer managed accounts require at least a $5,000 deposit. Most others require between $10,000 and $50,000 to open an account.

Many also limit access to the account to once a month on a specified day of the month. You may also be required to give a written notice several days before the last trading day of the month in which you want to withdraw funds in order to be allowed to take out your money.

You cannot easily move in and out of many managed accounts. Many limit the frequency with which you can enter or exit the system. Others require advance notice when you want to take out funds. Be sure you understand the rules for withdrawal before you deposit any money in a trading system account.

When you read the fine print on a managed account contract, be certain you understand the fees that you will pay, the minimum deposit you must maintain, and any limitations you might have on withdrawing your money. You don't want to be in a position of not having access to your money when you need it.

Trading Systems

Trading systems are a way to put your account on automatic pilot and let the system take over. They can be a good option for traders who may be too busy or overwhelmed to actively trade in the Forex market.

Trading systems will offer various trading strategies. Be sure you understand the trading strategies that are automatically programmed into the system you choose. You will find some trading systems that offer aggressive trading strategies, which signal you to take on high risk for a higher profit potential. You'll also find others that are more conservative.

While you don't have the potential to make as much with a more conservative system, your losses should also be minimized.

No matter what anyone tells you, no trading system can guarantee profits. Many trading systems signal to you when to buy and sell various Forex pairs. Others automatically handle the trades for you.

You will find promises of incredible trading wins based on hypothetical results. Hypothetical results are not based on a real portfolio trading with real money. They instead are trading simulations using historical price data. The trading system promoter can pick the best results using the best part of historical data for his system. So don't depend on impressive trading results that are based on hypothetical trading data.

Hypothetical trading results are like depending on 20/20 hindsight. Don't we all wish we could do that sometimes? That would give us the chance to correct mistakes by knowing what we know today. Unfortunately, the world doesn't work that way.

You may also see the words that the system is tested using real-time trading. Beware! That doesn't mean that real money was traded. It just means that the system was tested using a live data feed rather than with historical market data.

Fees for trading systems and managed accounts vary greatly, but can be as high as 20 percent on trading gains, as well as an annual fee of 1 to 2 percent of your account value. Be certain to read the fine print before signing any contract for a trading system, and make sure you understand the fees you will be charged for the services you will receive.

Managed Forex can be a good alternative if you don't have the time to spend researching the market and learning the trading tools. But you still need to carefully research any of the managers, managed accounts, or trading systems you choose to use. There are many scam artists out there that promise you huge profits with very little risk. Don't believe them. There is no risk-free way to trade Forex.

Fraud & the Forex (and how to avoid it)

You may hear get-rich-quick promises in late-night television ads or infomercials. You may also see promotions about ways to get rich quick on the Internet by trading in foreign currency. Don't believe any of them. Forex trading is risky and requires a significant amount of time to learn to do properly. Avoid getting caught up in Forex fraud schemes. In this chapter, we talk about the common types of fraud claims you might see and what you can do to protect yourself from becoming a victim.

Forex scammers use many different types of phrases to lure you in and make you think you can get rich quick. Your parents probably told you if something sounds too good to be true, it probably is. Remember that phrase as you read any offer to trade Forex.

You must be even more aware of scams if you suddenly acquired a large sum of cash from an inheritance, insurance settlement, or retirement funds that could attract fraudulent operators. Once the money is gone, it's very difficult, if not impossible, to recover.

We review some of the key claims you may hear via phone, mail, or e-mail. These claims were gathered by the United States Commodity Futures Trading Commission (CFTC) during their investigations of fraudulent Forex operators.

Claims Predicting Large Profits

Be cautious whenever you hear or read these claims:

- "Whether the market moves up or down in the currency market, you will make a profit."

- "Make $1,000 per week, every week."

- "We are outperforming 90 percent of domestic investments."

- "The main advantage of the Forex markets is that there is no bear market."

- "We guarantee you will make at least 30-40 percent rate of return within two months."

You should be careful anytime someone promises you extremely high performance.

Usually these claims are false.

Claims Promising No Risk

Anytime someone encourages you to trade Forex with a claim that there is little or no financial risk, it's false. Here are some common claims the CFTC has seen in fraudulent scams:

• "With a $10,000 deposit, the maximum you can lose is $200 to $250 per day."

• "We promise to recover any losses you have."

• "Your investment is secure."

Any attempt made by a company to downplay the risks you will take trading Forex is likely a scam. Don't trust anyone who tells you that the written risk disclosure statement you see in the mailing you received or on their website you are reading is just a required formality of a government agency.

You must accept that the currency markets are volatile and risks can be substantial, especially for inexperienced customers. Scammers look for unsuspecting folks who will deposit their money and quickly lose it.

Be Cautious About Trading Online

While you will find reputable firms that do offer online trading services, be sure you know a lot more about the firm you will be using for online trading other than what is on their website. Once you send funds electronically, it will likely be impossible to get them back if you later find out that the company is a fraudulent operator.

An enticing Internet site can look very professional. But remember it can cost an Internet advertiser just pennies per day to reach a potential audience of millions of people. Fraudulent currency trading firms have learned that the Internet is an inexpensive and effective way to reach a large pool of potential customers.

Scams Targeting Ethnic Minorities

Some Forex scammers find that a great way to get new customers is to target people in ethnic communities. The CFTC found that people in Russian, Chinese, and Indian immigrant communities are targeted through advertisements in their ethnic newspapers and through television "infomercials" on stations that serve those communities.

Sophisticated fraud operators may give you a beautifully designed glossy brochure with

impressive-looking charts. Don't depend on it. The information may be false. Always research a firm's claims no matter how good the information looks.

One common scam used in these communities is to advertise as though the company is offering you a "job opportunity" for an "account executive" to trade foreign currencies. When you get to the job, you find out that you must use your own money for trading. You likely will also be encouraged to recruit family and friends. You could be lured into a trap not only to lose your own money, but to encourage your family members and friends to lose theirs.

Don't Open an Account If You Can't Check a Firm's Background

Any firm that won't give you enough information to check their background is probably a fraudulent operator. Don't just accept the information you're given; be sure to carefully check it all out with the regulatory agencies.

When you do get information about a firm's background, don't depend on verbal statements you get from its employees. Be sure you get all the information in written form.

If you are not able to verify the information you are given, it's a sure sign you're dealing with a questionable firm. Don't do business with any firm that you can't prove is legitimate.

Don't Make Quick Decisions

A favorite tactic of many Forex scammers is to tell you by phone or e-mail that you must respond within a number of minutes or hours in order to get the deal promised. Don't fall for that tactic.

You should always take the time to research the firm that approached you. You should be sure that the firm is legitimate and one that you would be comfortable using as your broker.

Also, you should always research any tip or idea independently yourself. If you don't understand the tip or why it's worth acting upon, don't take the action.

Get Everything in Writing

You may hate to read the fine print, but be sure you get everything that is promised tomyou in writing. Read all documentation carefully and be sure that you understand what is being said.

Before opening an account, you should get a contract that spells out all the trading rules, referred to as the customer or account agreement. You should also get a risk disclosure statement that clearly spells out the risks of trading Forex.

In the customer or account agreement, you should find details about the laws and regulations under which the firm operates, the deposit requirements, details about trading on margin, and what happens if your account falls short. You should get information on how trades will be liquidated.

You should also get a full listing of services provided and any fees and charges for those services. Be sure that you understand all fees and the basis for each of these charges.

If you do plan to trade online, there will likely be a separate agreement for electronic order entry and access that spells out how to access your account online and how it will be managed.

Your entire relationship with your Forex broker will be governed by this customer or account agreement. Be sure you understand your rights and responsibilities, as well as the firm's rights and responsibilities, before signing anything.

If you don't understand something, ask about it and be sure that you do understand all provisions before signing the document. If the answer seems to differ from what you are seeing, be sure you get all promises in writing.

Avoid Any Money Manager That Won't Give You a Performance Track Record

If you choose to go with a money manager to handle your Forex account, you should always seek as much information as you can about their past performance. But be aware that the information you receive may not always be reliable, and can be very difficult to verify. Fraudulent money managers have been found to indicate that their performance track record is audited by an independent accounting firm, even though that information in itself is fraudulent.

Money managers are not required to provide this information, but be leery of any that refuse to give you information about its performance track record. And, of course, always look for a money manager with a long history of a reliable positive performance record.

Remember that anything a salesperson promises may not actually be honored if you don't get it in writing. If a salesperson hedges on putting something in writing, the claim likely is not true.

Seek Professional Advice from an Independent Third Party

It's always a good idea to seek advice from an independent third party that won't benefit financially from your decision to do business with a firm, especially when you are thinking of risking a lot of money. If you do want to get involved in Forex trading, talk with your local banker or accountant. He may be able to recommend a number of good firms to work with or possibly even a contact within your own bank. You don't have to work with your bank, but it can't hurt to sit down and talk with someone as you gather information about your Forex trading options.

Don't Trade More Than You Can Afford to Lose

Rule number one for Forex trading is to never risk more than you can afford to lose. We know that we've said this numerous times in the guide, but it is the most important thing for you to remember as you enter the exciting world of Forex trading.

Forex Trading Formulas

The Benefit of Vantage Points

Everything has laid the foundation for you to start applying your skills but first I want to lay out the case for taking a broad approach to trading in the Forex. By a broad approach, I meant to look at different time frames to gain more opportunities for profiting in Forex trading, Yes, there is a going to be one time frame that appeals to you the most (daytrading, momentum trading, swing trading, position trading, etc.) but by broadening your view beyond one time frame, you'll gain the ability to read the trends in Forex more accurately but also have the ability to seize more opportunities.

Just as a skilled fund manager seeks to reduce his risk by spreading his capital among several stocks for diversification, you also want to spread your capital among different currencies but also several different time frames in order to reduce your risk. At the same time, you'll be able to create more opportunities for yourself by gaining different points-of-view from what is happening in the market.

Short-term price fluctuations may offer opportunities that intermediate-term time frames won't and vice versa. But you'll also be able to see what's going on in the larger time frames which will help you stay on the right side of the primary trend in play.

This also means that even if you stick to one type of trading formula, you'll still gain a greater understanding of the forces at play by having the ability to see what's happening at the different levels by having more tools to work with.

So, let's start with...

Short-Term Trading Strategies

These strategies are helpful for day traders. The ones we will discuss aren't specifically for only day trading, but they tend to be more beneficial to traders looking to enter and exit a currency pair in the same day. The trade could consist of a few minutes to a few hours.

High-Impact

We talked about economic sources in another section. However, there are several reports that come out every day that are published on a global level. Large movements tend to happen when a heavy impact report comes out.

You can check out the economic calendar to see what's getting released today. A popular one is the Bloomberg's economic calendar. Look for a red star that marks the high impact releases. You may have several red stars on any given day or just one to none at all.

Also keep an eye out for gold or yellow stars which indicate important news that can affect the market, as well.

Day traders are looking for spikes in price movement and there is no better place to get spikes than from the news reports.

Watch how the news affects the market a few times before trading the first time. You will find that the first few minutes are spiky and tend to fight for direction. This can be from a government pushing money through to get better transfer rates and stabilize the currency.

After a few minutes, the currency should settle on the trend it will be on. Once you have a confirmed trend, you can enter the trade if you wish.

This strategy relies on news and what you see happening with the trend. All technical analysis is out the window with these trades.

Pivot Points

This is a simple strategy that is tried and true. It's super easy to see how powerful pivotpoints are by picking a previous day and calculating the "next day's" pivot points to back test this idea. You will find they are very good estimators for support and resistance. First used by floor traders on equity exchanges, pivot points have proven to be useful in other markets, especially the Forex.

To calculate pivot points for today, you use the previous day's prices.

Previous day's high + previous day's low + previous day's close = "n"

Then divide "n" by 3 = the Pivot Point

To use pivot points to estimate the support and resistance for today, use the following calculations:

• Resistance 1 = (2 X Pivot Point) - Low from previous day

• Support 1 = (2 X Pivot Point) - High from previous day

• Resistance 2 = (Pivot Point - Support 1) + Resistance 1

• Support 2 = Pivot Point - (Resistance 1 - Support 1)

• Resistance 3 = (Pivot Point - Support 2) + Resistance 2

• Support 3 = Pivot Point - (Resistance 2 -

Support 2)

This will give you 3 resistance levels and 3 support levels. Each tier will give you less of a probability of price passing it. For example, the Euro was first introduced on October 12, 2006. Here are the 3 tiers and the number of times price has gone lower or higher.

- Lower than S1 892 times, or 44% of the time

- Higher than R1 853 times, or 42% of the time

- Lower than S2 342 times, or 17% of the time

- Higher than R2 354 times, or 17% of the time

- Lower than S3 63 times, or 3% of the time

- Higher than R3 52 times, or 3% of the time

If you know that only around 42% of the time the price breaks through resistance 1, you can sell before reaching that point. The benefit of knowing this information is that you can gauge potential support and resistance ahead of time. It's kind of a reference point to place stops and limits on. Probability can help you reduce risks, which is especially important when trading currencies with high leverage.

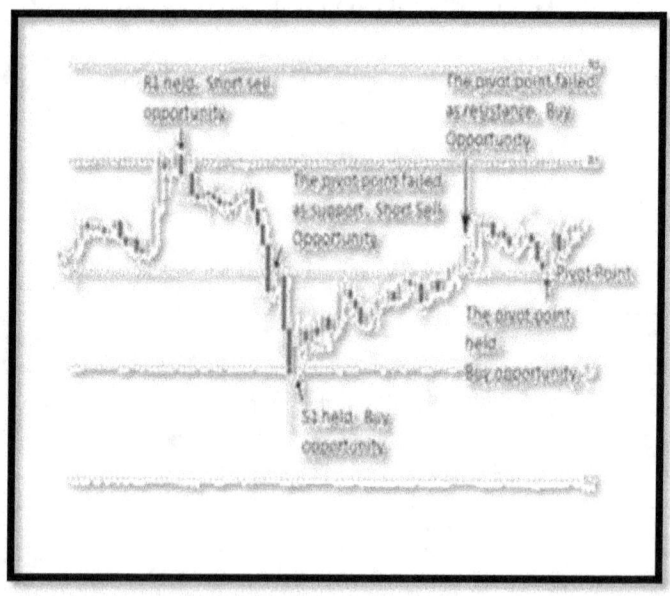

Gap Trading

In the stock market, when a company's earnings are higher than expected, the stock the next day may gap up if the news came out after hours. The stock would open higher the next day than it closed the day before.

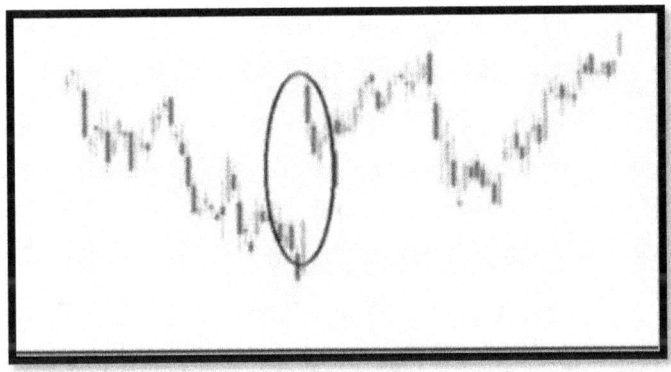

In the Forex market, news or reports can widen the bid and ask spread, making a gap.

Gaps come in four flavors in the Forex market (yum!).

• Common gaps can't be placed in a price pattern and represent an area where the price has spread.

• Breakaway gaps occur at the end of a price pattern and are strong signals of a new trend.

• Exhaustion gaps occur around the end of a price pattern and are signals at attempts to hit new highs and new lows.

• Continuation gaps occur in the middle of the price pattern signaling a lot of buyers or sellers.

When the gap gets filled, it comes back to the average level it was before the gap occurred.

There are three reasons this may occur:

•   Technical resistance is when the price moves up or down very sharply and doesn't have any support or resistance to fall back on.

•   Price patterns are used to classify gaps. For example, exhaustion gaps signal the end of a price trend and are likely to be filled. Breakaway gaps and continuation gaps are less likely to be filled since they confirm the direction of the current trend.

•   Irrational exuberance is when a price spike occurs from overly optimistic or pessimistic views, and are likely to fill the gap.

Fading refers to gaps that are filled the same day they occur. Day traders would be especially interested in gaps that fade. So let's discuss how you would take advantage of gaps in general.

•   Traders may look for news that favors a gap the next day. They will buy at odd hours when a report comes out late, in the hopes there will be a gap the following day. This is more of a swing type of trade but could be suitable for day traders as well.

•   Day traders look for high liquid positions early in a price movement hoping for a continued trend, buying a currency right as it starts to gap up with no resistance in sight.

- Day traders may look to short gaps once a high has been determined, especially if the gap was created by a speculative report.

- Traders may also buy when price levels reach the prior support after the gap gets filled.

Once a gap starts to get filled, it normally doesn't stop. This is due to the fact that there isn't any support or resistance around for it to use. In order for a gap to be considered a gap it needs to break key resistance levels on the 30-minute chart. To be considered filled, the price must retrace to the original resistance level.

On a candlestick chart, a gap on the Forex market may look like a large candlestick because it's a 24-hour market for most of the week (5pm EST Sunday to 4pm EST Friday). Gaps that look like stock market gaps will likely occur when the market opens at 5pm Sunday EST, but not always.

The trick to trading gaps is to know what caused the gap and how to correctly identify which type it is. Only then can you trade with a better probability of success. Gap trading is rather risky as is, but not understanding it fully is even riskier. During a gap there is low liquidity and lots of volatility.

Always use a stop loss during a gap. Prices can move fast and it can change before you have a chance to respond.

Momentum Rides

Riding momentum is about waiting for the market to have a surge of strength that will carry the currency in a trend (either up or down). The trader then jumps on the wave as it starts to form and rides it in. Once the wave starts losing momentum the trader jumps off and looks for another wave to catch. We've all seen surfing, so that's a great analogy, right?

Momentum trading looks for specific criteria and has a clear exit strategy. In order to find momentums you need to have the 20-period exponential moving average (EMA). The EMA makes a great way to track recent movements for fast trades. Use the moving average to find the trend and the moving average convergence divergence (MACD) histogram to help gauge momentum. Settings for the MACD should be 12,26,9 (default).

The idea is to wait for a reversal trade when the momentum supports it. Look for burst activity in a very small amount of time. Using five-minute charts works nicely. This is called the 5 Minute Forex momo trade.

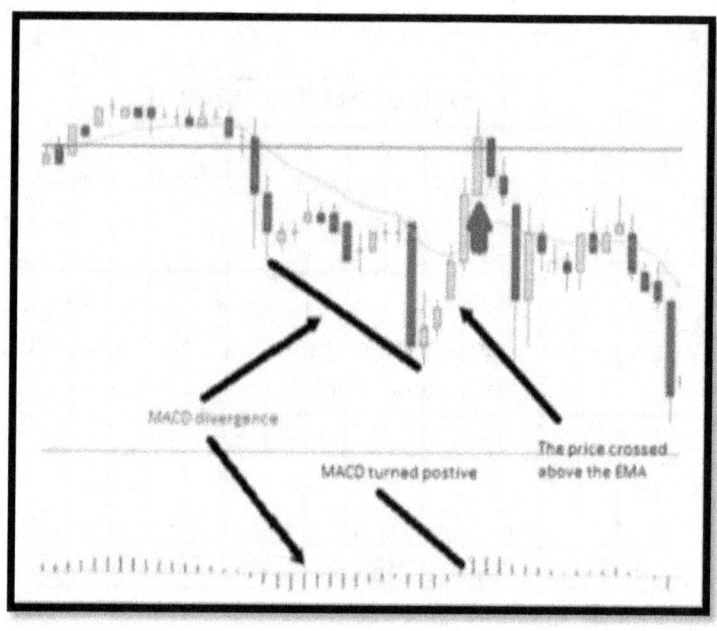

You want to look for a currency pair that is trading below the 20-period EMA and MACD to be negative. If the price crosses above the 20-period EMA, make sure that the MACD is in the process of crossing from negative to positive or has already done so.

To short trade, look for a currency pair to be trading above the 20-period EMA and for the MACD to be positive. When the price crosses below the 20-period EMA, check to make sure the MACD is in the process of crossing from positive to negative, or already crossed into the negative within the past five bars.

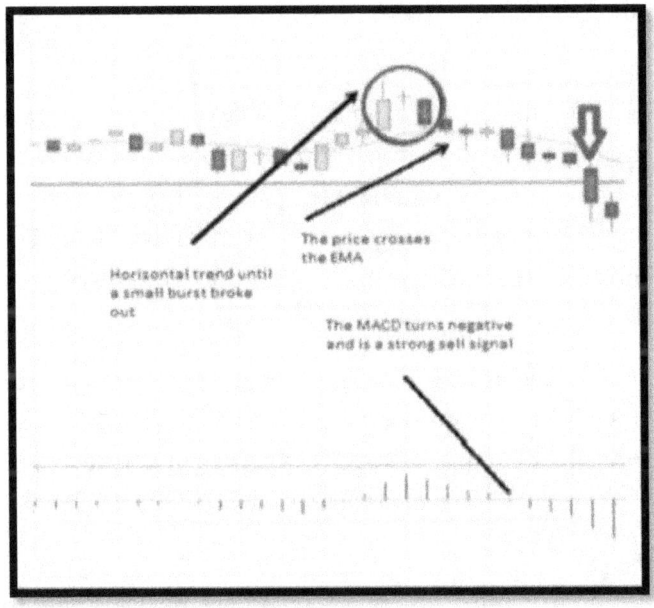

The price crosses the EMA

Horizontal trend until a small burst broke out

The MACD turns negative and is a strong sell signal

At the beginning of this discussion we talked about having a clear exit. The perfect exit is a two stage process. The first is at the point where you can lock in gains and ensure that the trade at least breaks even. The second exit is the remainder of the trade, which catches profits if the momentum takes off. Use stops to lock in breakeven points as well as to lock in profits as the currency moves.

Stop Hunting

Leverage for the Forex market is high. 100:1 is the default for most traders. It can be as high as 1000:1, though.

The insanely high degree of leverage in the Forex market is needed since currency moves by pips. In order to make money off a trade that went from 1.2023 to 1.2037, you need a lot of money. This can both be extremely profitable and ridiculously risky.

Retail traders can double their accounts in a day or lose it all. If you are in the Forex market as a day trader, you must use stops. With so much leverage, you simply won't last long without well placed stops.

As a day trader, you will tend to use that leverage to make profitable trades in a short amount of time. It's not good practice to sit a losing position out. You simply can't do that in a highly leveraged Forex position.

In fact, if a high leveraged Forex trade goes south and the trader tries to "sit it out," they can get a margin call, which is when the dealer requests that you deposit more money to recoup the lost funds. You may get forced into selling other positions and owing some money. Depending on how much leverage you used, this can get nasty pretty quickly.

With "stop losses" being taught to people left and right almost everyone uses them. What does this mean? Well, people like structure and round numbers. Most people are likely to place stops on round numbers. $1.0010 looks more appealing than $1.0013.

Stop hunting doesn't need to be just about stop orders. It could be for limit orders or stop orders alike.

Stop hunting involves flushing out the weak longs and the weak shorts. Large players like hedge funds and banks will push stops in the hope of generating more directional momentum.

The majority of stops are in numbers that end in round numbers. For example, a trade at $1.0284 in an upward trend would have most stops at $1.0290, while most large players place stops at more unusual locations, $1.0292 for example.

Let's pretend there are a ton of buy orders sitting at a specific price point.

If a price is approaching resistance, and just above the resistance is a nice round number, it will trigger a ton of buy orders pushing the trend up. Larger players (or brokers) can "trip" those orders to push the price up fast and sell at a large price.

Many of the regulations in place by the NFA and CFTC in the U.S. help stop brokers from doing things like this. But it still happens and it can still happen from large players in the market other than your broker.

Knowing it does happens allows you to position yourself better. On one hour charts, mark 15 pips above and below an approaching round number. This provides a 30 point area called the trade zone.

This helps you stay in a position without getting kicked out early.

For short positions, pushing a ton of stop losses will ensure the price continues to decline. With long positions, pushing buy orders will ensure the price rises more. 15 points ahead of the round number makes sure you exit when the big players do and don't get kicked out early.

Frogger

When you trade based on the right news release it can be highly profitable. Many jump right into the middle of the road which can get pretty hectic. This strategy is about playing the road like the game Frogger and looking for a pattern to form before jumping.

The largest rate movements in news for the Forex market is the non-farm payroll (NFP). As mentioned previously, this report has the total number of paid workers in the U.S. without farm employees and other agencies like government employees. When the news hits, it can cause some major movement.

The NFP gets released on the first Friday of every month at 8:30am EST. Most traders have found it better to let the news hit, wait for the volatility to die down and take a logical view on how the market is actually reacting than to guess or make trades in anticipation.

Sometimes the news can be good and the currency declines. Other times the news can be bad and the currency rises. Either way, the market is right. So instead of guessing, it's better to wait for a set-up and confirmation of trend.

The NFP report affects the USD the most, but has an impact on other currencies, as well. Those who stand back and reflect on what the news means and how it is affecting trades will be in a better position to ride the direction the market is now taking.

For this type of trade it's best to use 15-minute charts. If the news hits at 8:30am, the first bar will be between 8:30 and 8:45am. As a side note, the news doesn't always come on time so adjust accordingly.

The first bar in the first 15 minutes will be hectic. As you wait, you are looking for an inside bar formation to occur, which is a candlestick formation that has a price range falling within the previous bar's price range.

This represents indecision because no one seems to know where the trend will go.

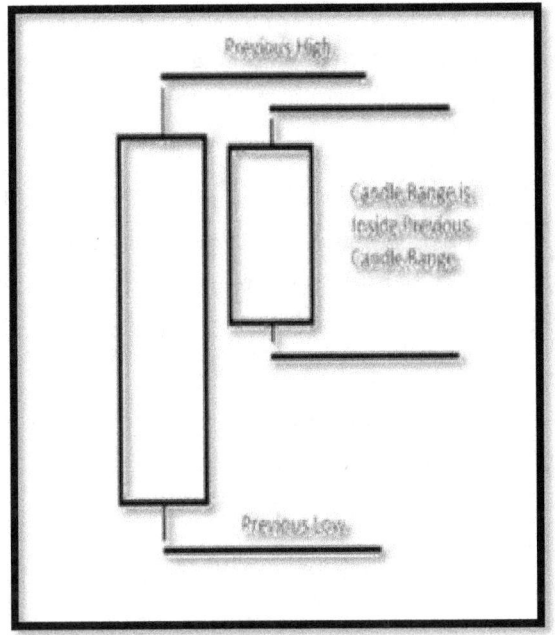

The inside candlestick's high and low are what we are paying attention to. These will probably be the deciding factors on the next trend. The next candlestick that closes above or below the inside candlestick's high or low is likely to be the next trend direction. This would be the entry point for either a long position or short.

If you back test this strategy you will find that most of the move ends after four hours. So always aim to exit your position before four hours hit. Trailing stops work great with this strategy since it frees you up in those four hours.

The inside candlestick formation doesn't need to occur in the beginning to be relevant; however, it should appear before you enter a position under this strategy.

Of course, anything is possible. The trend can change or the momentum could fade out.

Get familiar with historical NFP data and watch it a few times for practice.

Swing Trading Strategies

The swing trader is looking to hold a position for a day or two or more, taking advantage of trend situations. However, good swing trades in the Forex are hard to find. Hard, but not impossible, and once you get comfortable with what to look for, swing trades can be very profitable in currencies.

The fact that there aren't many entry signals to find means less risk when you find one that works.

The huge benefit swing trading has in the Forex is low risk. With day trading and investing you need a lot of capital to be profitable, not so much with swing trading. While the day traders and investors will typically have either large sums of capital or are large companies, the little niche in the middle of swing trading tends to be great for smaller retail traders. In fact, most successful retail traders in the Forex market are swing traders.

Trading with the Odds

Trading with the odds is about using technical input in which you would look for situations that have a lot of signals all pointing in the same direction, giving you a high probability that you will be profitable.

For swing trading, you rely on three types of candlestick charts. The first is the minute by minute, the second is the hourly, and the third is the daily. Here is a breakdown of the settings:

Minute by Minute

- RSI 15

- Stochastics 15,3,3

- MACD 12,26,9

Hourly

- EMA 100

- EMA 10

- EMA 5

- MACD 12,26,9 Daily

- SMA 100

It's also common for traders to use the following indicators:

- Trendlines

- Fibonacci retracements

- Arcs

- Fans

- Support and Resistance

- Pivot Points

The prefered method would be to have each of the three candlestick charts up at the same time in a side by side fashion on your monitor. This allows you to easily look for indicators from all three that point in the same direction.

You would look for trendlines that break out upwards, as well as positive divergences in RSI,

MACD and stochastics. Next you would look for moving average crossovers with the shorter crossing over longer, if the trend is moving toward a support and shows signs it will bounce back up.

For short positions, you would look for bearish candlestick engulfing formations. You would look for trendlines that break out downwards. As well as Negative divergences in RSI, stochastics, and MACD, along with moving average crossovers with the shorter crossing under the longer.

Relationship Strategy

All markets have correlations in them. One thing goes up and another goes down. Once you connect the dots you can predict, for example, that when the benchmark equities rise, bonds will fall.

There are relationships in the Forex as well. There is a very close relationship between the Australian dollar and gold, for instance. This is mostly because Australia is the largest producer of gold. To a lesser extent, China, South Africa and the United States are also producers of gold, but not as much as Australia. When gold production is up or down in Australia, the exchange rate will follow supply and demand.

Another strong relationship is the U.S. dollar and

crude oil. It's not because of productivity or use, but because the commodity in general is priced in dollars.

These relationships affect currencies over longer time frames. You could, but probably wouldn't want to, day trade on these correlations. These are much better suited for a few days to a week or more.

Currency pairs that move in the same direction (mostly) are:

EUR/USD and GBP/USD

EUR/USD and NZD/USD

USD/CHF and USD/JPY

AUD/USD and GBP/USD

AUD/USD and EUR/USD

Ones that move inversely (mostly) are:

EUR/USD and USD/CHF

GBP/USD and USD/JPY

GBP/USD and USD/CHF

AUD/USD and USD/CAD

AUD/USD and USD/JPY

You would use this information by not taking the same position for one pair that is inverse to the other. For example, you wouldn't short EUR/USD and USD/CHF. Since they normally move inversely, the chances of you profiting by shorting both is very slim.

When the stock market moves up, these pairs tend to move up:

- AUD/USD

- NZD/USD

- EUR/JPY

And, they move down when the stock market moves

down.

When the stock market moves up, these pairs tend to move down:

•   USD/CAD

•   EUR/AUD

•   GBP/AUD

And, they move up when the stock market moves down.

Oil affects currencies in different ways. For example, countries that export oil, like Canada, get hurt by declines in oil, while countries like Japan, who import oil, benefit.

Turn Trade Strategy

This strategy helps find turns in the price action using two main indicators on your charts, moving averages and Bollinger Bands (with 3 standard deviations). Bollinger Bands adjust themselves to market conditions using a standard deviation calculation.

The setup looks at daily charts with a 20-period SMA. This will give you a full month's worth of data and provide the average price. So, if the price action is above the average price, the trend is going up. If the price action is below the average price, the trend is going down.

To find an entry point, you would look at the hourly charts. Using the turn trade strategy, you look to trade in the direction of the trend by buying highly oversold prices in an uptrend and selling highly overbought prices in a downtrend.

To figure out if the currency was overbought or oversold, you would use Bollinger Bands. Use Bollinger Bands with 3 and 2 standard deviations on a daily chart, which is less volatile than the hourly charts. This type of strategy is for swing trades, so make sure you're using the right Bollinger Band settings on the right chart. You would increase the Bollinger Bands with a decrease in time frame. A five minute chart would use 4 standard deviations, for example.

Once you find the direction of the trend, you would observe the price action on the hourly chart. If the price continues to trade between the 3SD and the 2SD Bollinger Band this would indicate the momentum may take a nose dive.

If the price moves above the 2SD Bollinger Band you enter the market with a long position. You would ride the position until the pair closes out of the 3SD-2SD Bollinger Band which would mean the trend is over.

When placing a long position you want to make sure the price is above the 20-period SMA on the daily chart. You would then move to the hourly chart and place two pairs of Bollinger Bands for 3SD and 2SD. Buy at market price when the price breaks through and closes above the lower 3SD-2SD Bollinger Band. Set your stop loss. Set the first profit target at 50% of your risk. If you are risking 20 points, then take profits at 10 points above your entry. Move your stop loss up to that new break even point and prepare to exit the position when the price closes below the upper 3SD-2SD Bollinger Band.

For short positions on a daily chart, use a 20-period SMA and make sure the price is below that line. On the hourly chart, place two pairs of Bollinger Bands at 3SD and 2SD. Wait for the price to break through and close above the upper 3SD-2SD Bollinger Band on the hourly chart and sell at market. Set your stop loss. Set your first profit target at 50% risk. So if you are risking 20 points, then set your first limit order at 10 points above entry. Move your stop up to that new point. Your final exit should be when the price closes above the lower 3SD-2SD Bollinger Band.

Long-Term Trading Strategies

When the Forex was first created, it was only available to governments, banks and large hedge funds. Retail traders can now take part and see the kinds of profits the other players had for so long.

Investing is the process of looking at a currency pair over different periods of time. The setup for long term investments lasting a year or more typically looks at three time periods. Monthly, quarterly and yearly. Using less then three seems to limit the long term view and more than 3 tends to provide too much data.

When looking at an investment for a year or more, it's best to start your study of the charts as far out as possible and work your way down to understand where the currency has been and where it's going.

Monitor the major economic news and trends. Any developments should be monitored to assess if it's a threat to your long term trade or not.

Another variable with long time frames is interest rates. We talk about this more in "carry trades," but normally, capital will flow toward the currency with the higher rate in a pair since this means better returns on the investment.

Interest Analysis

It's important to understand the market sentiment, which means the emotions and feelings of the people trading in the currency market. This section talks about how to assess market sentiment using interest analysis.

The Forex market doesn't provide volume because all the transactions are "over the counter" and aren't done through exchanges like other markets. There isn't a record of the transactions that have already taken place or of the ones that are currently taking place. Without volume as an indicator, the next best thing is open interest data on currency futures.

There is volume data on currency futures which help you measure a market. The largest exchange, the Chicago Mercantile Exchange (CME), handles currency futures. Currency futures are based on contract sizes with durations of three months.

Currency futures are quoted (mostly) in foreign currency against the U.S. dollar. In the Forex you would see a pair like USD/CHF and in currency futures you would see CHF/USD.

If the Swiss franc (CHF) depreciates against the U.S. dollar, the USD/CHF will rise and the Swiss franc future will decline. Some futures are quoted the same in both markets. For example, in the Forex you have EUR/USD and the euro futures are also EUR/USD. If the euro rises as EUR/USD, then both go up.

When looking at the currency alone and not in a pair, they tend to move together in both the Forex and futures. When a currency goes up, it will go up across the board. If GBP appreciates, the GBP/USD future will go up. But let's say that CHF appreciated, then the Forex USD/CHF will go down since CHF increases in strength.

Open interest is the total amount of contracts entered into the system that have not been delivered yet. These are contracts that are still outstanding waiting to be delivered.

When open interest increases it's because speculators are trading more aggressively in the market. An increase in open interest supports the current trend and lends strength to its continuation. When open interest decreases it means speculators are pulling money out of the market.

In a perfect uptrend or downtrend open interest should increase. In an uptrend increase, open interest means that long positions are in control, and in a downtrend, an increase in open interest means short positions are in control.

If the open interest decreases it could mean the momentum is coming to an end.

Open interest is a strong indicator for investors riding an uptrend. Over the long term, the investor would watch open interest to judge when the trend is ending to exit the position. Open interest works very well on a three month chart.

COT Report

Commitments of Traders (COT) is a report that started in 1962 covering agricultural commodities, then it slowly started adding additional information to its lineup and now covers foreign currency futures every week. Sounds great, right? Well, the data that gets released is delayed by three business days since it's published every Friday for the previous Tuesday's contracts. So it's not a huge help to a day trader, but for an investor it can provide a strong way to gauge price action.

You can go directly to the U.S. Commodity Futures Trading Commission's website to check out the Commitments of Traders market report.

The trick is to separate the important information from the not so important. Here is what to look for:

Long Report - This report includes where the big players are holding positions.

Open Interest - This report will give you the futures contracts not yet offset.

Number of Traders - The traders who are required to report positions to the CFTC are listed here.

Non Reportable Positions - Both long and short open-interest positions that don't meet the reportable requirements.

Reportable Positions - All futures and options that are held above certain reporting levels.

Spreading - A report that measures the extent of non-commercial trading holds equal long and short futures positions.

Most commercial currency trading is done in the spot market and not in futures. Commercial futures positions aren't likely to give accurate measures of what's happening in the spot market. However, where the COT report shines is in the noncommercial data. This data shows accurate positions from traders in the market.

When you see in the COT report that market positions are flipping, it's a strong signal to trending changes. When you see very extreme positioning in the currency futures market, it represents reversals. The reason for the reversal is because when there are so many speculators weighted in one direction, there is no one left to buy or sell. Monitoring the open interest can be used to figure out the strength of a trend.

Carry Trade Strategy

A carry trade is one of the more popular trades in the currency market. It's a favorite strategy of large hedge funds as well as retail traders. To "carry" a trade you rely on the interest rate. Each currency has a short-term interest rate that is set by the bank of the country it's from.

You buy a currency with a high interest rate and use a currency with a low interest rate to purchase it. The down side to carry trades is that once the trend starts to waiver, the decline can be aggressive. It's called carry trade liquidation and happens when traders and large companies feel the ride is over and look to sell. Bids disappear and the profits from interest rate differentials aren't enough to offset capital losses.

The entry point for a carry trade is right when the rate-tightening cycle starts. Buy a high yielding currency. Fund it with a low yield currency. You can find the current interest rates by visiting the website of the central bank of the country

Why is this such a popular strategy? For example, Australian dollar/Japanese yen AUD/JPY offers, on average, an annual interest of around 5%. That can be looked at as a low interest rate, but with the leverage power of currency trading that can turn into some very high profits.

Watch for central banks looking to increase interest rates, either doing so or planning to do so. The power of a carry trade looks at high yield as well as increasing yield. The benefit is in the yield as well as the appreciation.

When a central bank raises interest rates, the players (large companies and retail traders alike) take notice. The result of everyone jumping on the bandwagon is a push in value to the currency pair. The trick is to get in at the beginning of the cycle.

In environments that are low volatility, a carry trade can still be profitable. In fact, even if the currency doesn't move a cent, they still earn the leveraged yield.

The risks with carry trades is when a central bank reduces interest rates.

When they do, investors will likely leave in favor of another trade. The more drastic the reduction in interest rates, the more likely investors will move on.

The trade isn't worth it when the exchange rate is devalued by more than the average annual yield.

Central banks can also step in and prevent their currency from rising or falling. For example, a currency can get so high it starts affecting exports, while a weak currency could really hurt countries with a lot of foreign operations.

It's a long-term strategy and not something you would hold for a day or two. People tend to hold for months to many years with long positions.

Manage Your Trades

The Forex market is not a wheel of fortune where you can simply place your bets with sure winnings, big or small. The Forex market is dynamic and fluid; in a single blink of an eye, new information and prices develop thereby creating new opportunities for Forex market traders and changing previous expectations.

The bottom line is this: a foreign exchange market trader can optimize his trading strategy by making sure that he thoroughly plans each trade before getting affected by his emotions. In this way, he can improve his overall chances of taking profits and gains while minimizing the risks and losses.

If you are following a medium to long term foreign exchange trading strategy, it would be best if you use wider take profit limits and stop loss orders. However, it would be a good idea if you stay on top of the market at all times, even if you are a long term Forex market trader, since a lot can happen between the time you open and close a position. Unexpected events that can affect your positions may come at the most inopportune time.

A key point here: every Forex market trading strategy needs to take into consideration future events, public policy, news, and other relevant data even before a position is opened. Hence, a prudent Forex market trader will gather and take note of all the data and information available before he trades.

Evaluate Your Trading Results

In evaluating the outcome of any trade, it would be very beneficial if you look back over the whole process of opening and closing a position, as well as the time in between - regardless of the pips that you gained or lost. In this way, you will be able to understand what you did right and what you did wrong. Some key questions you can ask yourself are the following:

1.   How did I identify the trading opportunity?

2.   Did I take advantage of that trading opportunity?

3.   What trading method did I use to gain the most pips or profits in a day or week or month or

year?

4.   How well did the original trading plan work out?

5.   Was I able to monitor the market while my positions are open?

You have everything to gain and nothing to lose in this scenario. For instance, you can identify your good points and what you are not so good at, and adjust your Forex market trading approach and methodologies accordingly. Evaluating your foreign exchange market trading results on a daily, weekly, monthly or yearly basis is a crucial step in improving your trading acumen and diminishing your trading losses.

Final Words

There are many traders that buy Forex signal systems, which are packages that help traders make trades. These systems offer trend, range and fundamental signals.

Trading in a trend is all about predicting future movement based on past data, while range trading is all about support and resistance levels using technical analysis. The type of system you use will work best if it's for the right market. Range systems will work best in range markets and trend systems work best in trending markets. If you buy a signal system, make sure it doesn't favor one or the other. Some may be mostly range or mostly trend, which is OK if that's what you want.

A fun part of trading is that everyone does it a little differently. You can use a number of factors to find your style and what works for you. Successful trading uses a combination of technical and fundamental analysis.

It's always best to "practice" with demo software instead of just jumping in. You should practice your system before using it live. You will find your system of trading is an ongoing activity with small improvements made along the way. Work out the major kinks first with a demo account. Your broker will probably provide a demo account or software. If not, find one that does. You can also find demo or virtual trading accounts online. But it's best to use the one provided by your broker so you can practice with the software you plan to use when you start a real account.

You may find the software platform is not to your liking. It's better to find that out with a demo account than an active account. Demo accounts will have exactly the same look and function as active accounts. The only difference is fake money vs real money.

The demo account is practice for you to perfect a specific strategy. Your strategy is your system. It's best to stick with one currency pair to learn how it moves in the market. Become comfortable with how it responds to news. Apply your system the same way every time. If you want to make changes (and you should) you do it when not holding a position.

If you allow yourself to make gut feeling decisions on the fly, you're going to lose your account. Without experience to back it up, it's almost always the wrong move.

It's been said you can give one trader money to go long on a stock and another trader money to go short on the same stock and they will both lose money. It's true if they don't have a solid system that they stick to, and all their decisions are based on guesses and betting.

When you find indicators and technical analyses that give you high probabilities in one currency pair while learning to implement stop losses and exit points, you start to nail down a solid system.

Even then, that $400 a day (day trading) and $1500 a week (swing trading) in the demo account turns to $250 a day and $1000 a week when transferred over to an active account. You will have bad days and bad weeks.

Call it a day (or week) if you see a trend. The market can act in ways you aren't familiar with, which make great days to work your demo account.

I hope you have a clear understanding of how the Forex trading system works and how to make money using it. Implement the strategies laid out in this guide and begin to reap the rewards.

Good luck!